'There are two journeys in this book. One is the astonishing physical feat of circumnavigating the globe on a Triumph motorcycle faster than anyone before, a story of intense hardship and fatigue in the face of daunting barriers and overwhelming odds. The second is an extension into the mind, where Nick's ability to skim the superfluous and seize on the significant opens fascinating doors into the human condition. There are insights here which apply to us all and not just such driven adventurers as Nick. There is too a deep irony underlying this book, which documents Nick racing around the world to find out why he is racing around the world.

It's this multi-layered narrative, so incisively written, which makes Fastest Man Around the World such a compelling read.'

Kevin Ash
Motorcycling Correspondent
Daily Telegraph

By the same author

Non-fiction
Journey to the Source of the Nile
22 Days Around the Coast of Britain
The Great Bike Ride
Short Summer in South America
Bicycle : Image and the Dream

Videos
Longest Narrow Boat Journey in the World
Black Sea Odyssey
Fastest Man Around the World
Kaleidoscope Coast
Journey to the Top of the World
American Dream
Journey to the Edge of the Sahara
4 Go To Europe
The Emerald Way
Road Head
Global Rider Series parts I to IV

If you would like to purchase any of the above titles please go to:
www.nicksanders.com
If you would like to participate on any of Nick's Moto Challenge tours,
please go to:
www.motochallenge.com

Nick Sanders

Fastest
Man
Around
The
World

On the Road Books

An On the Road Book

P.O.Box 27 Machynlleth Powys SY20 8WT

www.nicksanders.com

www.motochallenge.com

First published in Great Britain by **On the Road Books,** 1999

2nd Edition (revised) 2003

Set in 10 / 11pt Times New Roman
Layout by Cyberspace
Printed and bound in Great Britain by
Cox & Wyman, Reading

ISBN 0 9537290 0-1

ACKNOWLEDGEMENTS

If it wasn't for the following people this journey would not have happened and I want to thank them all for their trust and support.

THANKS TO: Nick Gregg and Peter White at Mobil Oil (UK). Bruno Tagliaferri and Charles Smart at Triumph (UK). Jonathan Fleet at IBM Global Network. Noni and Fraser at FM Scottoiler. Jackie and Helen at Palmerston Travel. Fiona and Madrin at Wyndham Leigh PR. Eric and Pam at FM Television. The Triumph dealers in Istanbul, Perth, Anchorage and San Antonio. Dr. Greg for the lamb chops and the poem. Boz for the e-mails.

Special thanks to Antony Freeman for editing and proof reading the manuscript and for his superb revision. Also to my late and much loved Dad who I hope is watching over me. And as ever, my wife Hennie, because she is always with me.

ABOUT THE AUTHOR

Nick Sanders is one of the most versatile adventurers in the UK and one of the most experienced adventure bikers in the world. He has now ridden a motorcycle around the world four times, the second time in a record-breaking 31 days 20 hours. He has motorcycled the length of the Americas from Tierra del Fuego to Alaska (30 days) and has led several group expeditions, most recently taking 22 riders around the world on his 30,000 mile Motorcycle World Challenge. In 2002 he rode twice around the world – 50,000 miles on a Yamaha R1. He has also cycled around the world twice, the first time in 138 days and the second time in 79 days, setting a new record each time. He has cycled to Timbuktu across the Sahara, cycled the length of South America, cycled along the course of the White Nile and then through 80 countries. He has taken two English canal narrow boats to the Black Sea and back. He is also a microlight pilot and balloonist. Nick Sanders lives with his wife Henrietta and three children in a farmhouse in Wales.

For Hennie, Willow, JJ and Tatty

1

I made it to Sambalpur in the dark and checked into a hotel. The shabby walls of my room were encrusted with bad paint. The cream-coloured telephone and Formica-topped television made a pretence to modernity, when in reality the place looked tragic and second hand, a room abused by a thousand strangers.

The place depressed me with its morbid dinginess. I was to sleep here for five hours with the cockroaches before rising to ride again in the dark. I was desperately tired. I needed a very long sleep. But there wasn't time. I was trapped between wanting to be home and wanting to be far away.

My bike was parked in the hotel lockup. The engine was still cooling when my head hit the pillow. I dreamed I was standing by the bike somewhere in an Indian desert. It was in Maharastra. It reminded me of a time before, when I had been overwhelmed by the endlessness of the Sahara and the heat of the Thar Desert.

Desert heat had the trick of making clocks stand still for travellers. During the day the sharpness of the horizon was diluted by the shimmering air, and the will to voyage was diminished by the coolness of the shadows. Everywhere was brown. Brown mountains and brown trees, brown people with sandy-coloured dogs, and a brownness in the baked air.

"I have bicycled around the world twice. I have motor-biked around the world twice. Tell me, mind, does not passing the same places twice give me the validity I search for?"

"Probably not," answered my mind, *"because the reason for doing it again is that you were not aware of the experience the first time."*

"How many times do I have to be a journeyman around this planet before I can believe that I am solid and exist; before I know where I am going and why? One day I will be old and have to stay at home, and then it will be too late."

"Just once. If you go round and round a hundred times and experience only time and distance, then it will be as if you never went at all. The journeying will have been wasted. But if you are fully aware of the journey, the cycle of unknowing can be broken. If you sleep through your experiences, then how can you learn through your suffering not to have to suffer again? Not to know is not to suffer and not to suffer is not to learn. This is the basis of all religions. It is a law of life. It is something you have to understand before you can start any journey."

But maybe these thoughts were not from a dream. Perhaps they had come from a conversation on the terrace of a café, overlooking some icon of the world that I had barely given a second glance.

I sat up in my bed and looked wearily around at the nicotine-stained wallpaper which, on the ceiling, was the colour of sick. I remembered riding the bike in the night across Orissa to get here, twisting and turning through the forests and the bandits, and before that to Nagpur, and before that from Bombay, and all since two dawns ago.

I lay down again to sleep and lurid pictures flashed into my mind, a bedlam of the old and insane and beggars and people with the pox. Then with his round spectacles and grey Oxford moustache, an old man called Mr Fares strode across the inside of my head. I remember him. He owned the Golden Hotel in Talaat Herb Street off Tahrir Square. I was in Cairo. It was 1983. I was walking through the market in Bab al Luk, past the Falafel restaurant and up his shabby stairs.

"It's all very well to go around the world," he told me, "but you don't in fact need to go except to realise that this is so." He was eighty years old and he made me see the uselessness of my task. For the next sixteen years I was to struggle to make sense out of something that in his terms was quite senseless. "It is all here, here," he said, remonstrating with his spindly old man's arms. "It is here in front of you, before your nose. That is life, eh?"

2

In a place far away from Sambalpur, in a village in England near where I once lived, the village hall from time to time turned into a small cinema. A screen was put up and a projector was installed, and enthusiasts ran 16mm films. Maurice was a member of the committee. He was a psychoanalyst, and had a London practice which he operated three days a week. He looked like a Benedictine monk, with his remaining hair skirting the top of his head. His heavily-lensed glasses gave you the confidence to look him in the eye because his pupils were blurred.

I once said to Maurice at a film night: "You know, every day of my life someone comes up to me and tells me I need to see someone like you. Nicely though, they're not meaning to be unkind. They just say it because of what I do. What do you think?" I wanted to know because he represented the professional angle. How often do you meet a shrink in real life?

The film we watched that night was called 'Ma Vie en Rose'. It was about a boy who thought he was a girl. I too had a confusion, not about my gender but about what kind of adventurer I was and whether I was one at all. My explorer-adventurer-recordbreaker-sportsman-type persona had long since blurred. I didn't even know why I did it any more. To motorbike around the world faster than anyone had thought possible was sort of newsworthy, but really, what was the story? Stuck on my bike day and night, I was to pass a planet full of people and yet speak to only a few of them. Crammed inside my helmet, I heard only the sound of my engine mixed with the noise of surrounding traffic.

You would think it would be exciting, racing across continents to capture an obscure world record, but in my helmet I was alone with my thoughts as places and colours and vital smells rushed past before I could breathe them in. India looked interesting but suddenly I wasn't there any more. Thailand was brown. Malaysia was dark because I rode through it at night. Singapore was busy.

Then I realised, somewhere along the way, that it was all too much for me to take in. This journey, made up of a million disconnected parts, was driving me mad. Maurice the psychoanalyst had taken just a little too long to convince me that everyone else wasn't right. Maybe he thought I was a little bit crazy. If so, surely there had to be some way to absolve myself from this diagnosis.

"So what did you do?"

"I created another person in my head and had conversations with him."

"To prove that you weren't mad? What was the point of that?"

"It kept me awake for a start, because it was really tedious being on the road. And also he asked the right questions. When people asked me questions they usually asked the wrong ones."

"Such as?"

"Oh, they'd ask like, how did I get across the oceans..."

"And...?"

11

"In a goddamm submarine, what do you think? I mean come on."

"That's a bit harsh, it's only people being friendly. You wouldn't like it if they ignored you."

"Maybe, but after you've just ridden through jungles and plains and little country roads and someone comes up and asks you what you're doing and you say going around the world in under thirty-three days and they say *'What, on that?!'* Well of course *on that* – what else? I mean, am I being a bit hard?"

"I think you are. You sound very angry."

"I-AM-NOT-ANGRY. Or maybe I am. But while we're at it, who the hell are you?"

"I'm your alter ego, mate. I guess I'm you. I'm a genie in a bottle which you've just uncorked. I don't wear a crash helmet but I'm inside yours. Voices in yer head, mate."

3

The journey started one Spring morning at the Pagoda in Battersea Park, London. Around me were my sponsors and a lot of people from the newspapers, and there was a giant ramp which I was supposed to ride down. I said goodbye to Henrietta. We kissed tenderly and I promised that she would forever be the girl of my dreams, and that I wanted to be with her until I died. This could be years or weeks. Then off I rode, barely missing the toes of Peter the Sponsorship Manager who hastily stepped back, his chin squeezed against his neck. 'Day 1, *Sponsor Flattened by Round the World Biker.*'

The bike was a 900cc Triumph Daytona. It had no special preparation for the journey except for the mounting of a Scottoiler chain lubricating system and a tracking device. I carried no tools except a wheel spanner and no spare parts other than a chain. I took as little equipment as possible which was about as much as I needed, although I would have been better prepared with more. I had two saddle bags containing a small summer sleeping bag, laptop computer, mobile phone, small video camera and tapes, passport and money. I took no spare clothing and wore the same clothes from start to finish. That meant that most evenings I washed the one set I was wearing in the hotel sink.

It was inevitable that on the first day I would fall behind schedule. However well-planned an expedition may be, the two weeks before departure are always frantic. I hardly slept during the last three nights. By the time I reached the press call at Battersea Park I was already very tired, and when I reached France I was not really in a fit state to start riding around the world. Then a short way outside Calais I ran out of petrol and I had to lock my bike to a motorway barrier and hitch forty miles to get some fuel. For the remainder of this half-day I rode hard down the A26 to Reims, past Troyes and by evening into Chaumont, where I climbed into a small hotel bed by ten. I had ridden 382 miles, nearly 400 down by the end of the first day.

I slept until seven the next morning and was on the road before eight. It was a beautiful sunny morning with one of those electric blue skies that you read about in Himalayan romance novels. The forecast was for clouds and rain in the south. I set off late, not caring.

I was past Dijon within the hour, whizzing along the autoroute with abandon. I felt strong and fit. The bike sounded good, held the road well and faced into the wind sturdily. Sweet-smelling rapeseed pollen occasionally floated across the autoroute, and in the fields the truest yellow stretched against the bluest sky in a happy marriage of colour. The wind plundered thoughts from my helmet as it sucked out the air. The roar of the wind mixed with the noise of my engine. From the autoroute I caught glimpses of plaits of rapeseed not yet unfurled; farmers hosing down terraces of ripening vines, or sitting beneath terracotta eaves sipping wine. I felt happy. In my imagination I sat and drank with them, dozy in the quiet air. By the time the afternoon light had curdled, I was bloated with the day's efforts, and aching as I reached Aix en Provence.

I skirted Nice and Monaco on the Autoroute de Cote d'Azur. Customs at the border between France and Spain were friendly, and provided my only conversation of the day. "Hello Mister Customs Man, here is my passport, where can I change some money?"

I wanted to keep things simple. I had some experience of how such an adventure could become increasingly strange, but as I left customs, chucked my bags over my bike and sat astride, I never suspected how much the intensity of this journey was going to change me. It all sounded very straightforward, this fast, long-distance biking, but it wasn't.

You have to haul yourself across limits of physical endurance and across mental obstacles, and forget the concept of normality.

As I started that day's ride down the autoroute towards the south of France, I wondered at precisely what point in this world journey I would crack. After all, it had happened before. I once went AWOL on the Danube, and ran around babbling in the Nubia, so where would I lose it this time, and what would happen if my fingertip hold on reason were to slip?

As night falls I hurry on towards the Italian Alps, sharp-edged in the distance. I find a hotel and take only minutes to eat, mail my story and sink into a deep, shoulder-hugging bed. My bike is locked to a farm trailer by the hotel and I am locked in my room. My leathers are hung in the corner, looking almost like another man. They remind me of my other self. When I slip into my motorcycle clothing now, I have an alter ego for company. The shutters are open, overlooking a terrace with the kind of old sodium lights that bugs like to live in. Facing the steeple of the local church are empty seats made shiny by rain.

It was raining when I woke at four-thirty. I couldn't face getting up so early and plumped up my pillow for more sleep. Now I would have to ride to the late end of the day, but at least I had the option. Once I start riding the bike there are no more choices. I ride until dark in torrential rain, in snow, in crosswinds that make it hard to stay upright, and then have to keep riding for half the night.

The weakness of this journey is that the schedule is absolute. I am under pressure from my own boldness and tormented by the need to succeed. I am afraid for this journey because it is too fragile to sustain many problems. There will be no forgiveness for mistakes. One lesson I learned from my Pan-American adventure in 1996 was the need to ride hard from the very beginning; to accumulate mileage, not speculate on it. Yet already I am showing alarming signs of laziness. If I leave Europe for Asia only a few hundred miles down on my most optimistic schedule, more than half a day behind, then the time might not be regained until Australia or even America. It is only day three and everything to come still feels so far away.

Today the sky was covered with heavy clouds and rain poured down pipes and gutters and flowed along the road. Streams cascaded down the lower slopes of high mountains around the Col de Tende. Steep-sided valleys seemed to be rooted in place by a million tall, slender trees that were shaped to anchor heavy winter snow.

I set off fast, every few seconds down and up through the gears for yet another bend. Rain peppered down, sealing the edges of my helmet and making me gulp for air. Clutch in and out quickly to sandwich each change of gear, ten to a minute, sometimes sliding the back wheel on a patch of greasy road. Up through the gears, accelerating until the rain streamed down my visor - a quick wipe - more gears, leaning into the corner, around and up, more wipes and into the Col de Tende tunnel.

Orange neon lights stroked across my face. Half an hour later I had ridden through to the other side of Tende Mountain, where it was snowing. Scooped off bitterly cold peaks by a valley-funnelled wind, the rain had become swirling white flakes that were settling and making the road slippery. I was becoming chilled, and shivered whenever I stopped. Sweeping down the mountain and on to the plains of the River Po, east of the Piedmont, I rode with a following wind that kept pace with me, pushing me north.

Roof tiles of baked clay were wet and dark and looked the colour of ruby as the weather worsened and the light diminished. Visibility through my visor was poor. It was like peering through a steam bath and only the rivulets of rain water running down it gave me any clear view. The road was straight, narrow and the colour of sand. It was a Sunday, and in the villages and small towns of northern Italy families were dressed for church.

After joining Autoroute 6 south of Torino I made for Milan, before turning north again for Como and Lugano. The flat landscape was suddenly replaced by high-forested mountains and lakes, and these in turn were replaced by higher mountains that poked above the snow line. Low cloud started to let loose snow on a blustery wind. Every few moments of spring were stilled by a return of winter, and in slow Swiss traffic percolating from one tunnel to the next I reached midday with barely 250 miles more on the clock. I was acutely aware of the quickness of the passing of time and the slowness of the accumulation of distance.

In the Gotthard Tunnel, over ten miles long, the white light of the roof lamps streaked around and down my body like strobes. Deep underground, absorbed by this experience, it seemed to me that I was alive only as a reflection of moving parts. Then I rounded a bend and shot out of the tunnel into more snow. The wind blustered it into drifts across the road and across my visor. I had to stop and scrape the snow off my helmet while a gritter cleared the road.

Across Switzerland the weather presented me with the tail-end of winter, taunting me with one final snap of cold. Only when confronted with the furnace heat of India, later in the trip, would I long for such refrigerated cool. I continued towards the suburbs of Zurich and its bright red trains that looked like old ladies wheeling their shopping. I hardly noticed the city, bypassed the centre on a peripherique, and emerged into the wide, windy plains of Shaffhausen with a sea of snowy whiteness on either side of the road.

By Stuttgart I was chasing a setting sun and concentrated on riding at 130 miles per hour on an unrestricted stretch of German autobahn. The evening was dark and cold. I rode the final 200 miles to Regensburg in three hours. That meant I had ridden 703 miles since being in the Alps for breakfast. It had been a hard ride and I was not yet strong enough for the journey; by the time I rode into the city and found a hotel I was exhausted. When I climbed off the bike I could hardly stand, and it took me a few moments to straighten my legs. It's no wonder that sometimes in my dreams it is the morning after the night before and I am dead. I am a crusading fool, bereft of reason.

Diary: Thoughts before the following morning

I am in my bed at night. I have not yet woken. I hear the sound of wind against the eaves and imagine I see tumbleweed flicking against the window panes. Nothing inspires me to want to wake, get on my bike and ride for another day; except that I know I have a heart that sags without a quest. I snore quietly. My breath shows in the cold air of my dream. I sing in my sleep about the lilies where love once fed and remember soft, secret smiles. I cherish their taste like milk. In my suspended consciousness I know that she is now far away. I am not me but a spirit carried by strange winds.

I wake. The wind is still blowing. It is day four. A grey Monday in April. If it's Monday morning it must be Germany; if it's lunchtime this must be the Czech Republic; if it's late afternoon we're in Slovakia and by evening, welcome to Hungary. It is now two o'clock in the morning and I am still finishing off the day's business. I enjoy it, but the magic moments mingle with the sleepless nights and the fear of catastrophe.

It was three in the morning when I finished writing and e-mailing my reports. After four hours sleep and dreams of Patagonia, I drifted back into consciousness to find a blue sky shining through the net curtains to make love with my face.

It was a dry and beautiful day. I checked out and headed north towards Weiden within fifteen minutes of opening my eyes. After coffee in Weiden, where I stole glances at housewives and girls wearing pinnies, I carried on north-eastwards towards Prague. The rolling soft hills here wore a scattering of snow. I rode past stalls by the side of the road selling Charlie Chaplin garden gnomes, and entered the Czech Republic by early afternoon. All I saw was autoroutes, shopping malls and people rushing about in their cars.

I reached Prague and stood for half an hour by the Bridge of Sighs. The engine of the bike was hot and I was hot. An hour later I was on the autoroute to Brno, riding past the tramlines and tenement blocks, coursing a straight line across a landscape that was rural and clean. Smallholdings were proudly tidy and the whole countryside looked as if it was swept daily. By Bratislava I was wistful, at the Slovak-Hungarian border I was laughing with the guards. At nightfall I cruised into Budapest, looking for a friend's address from where I could work that night. My friends in Budapest compare their city with Chicago. East German tenors once sang Schubert in the Opera House there and tickets for the performances could be purchased for less than the cost of a croissant at today's prices.

It took me all morning to reach the Romanian border. Across the border in Romania the telegraph poles leaned over more, totems of a country that was economically bankrupt. All day it rained. Big raindrops fell hard, bursting on impact to raise a wall of spray through which I could just make out the road ahead. Beneath me on the road, sweeping tracks of cow shit and beetroot squashed by tractors threw the back end of the bike into skids, and it seemed that every minute there was the real chance of a crash. Eighteen hours multiplied by sixty minutes is a lot of missed chances, but I didn't fall.

I stopped for tea in a small roadside restaurant and I was told that food would not be ready for another hour, so I decided to ride on. Later, underneath a canopy of stars and dark space, I stopped to eat and sleep at the edge of a small forest. I climbed up wooden steps into a cabin, which was empty except for a waitress and a small man in the corner. After standing a while in front of a blazing log fire I took off my leathers to stop the flow of water to my boots from my neck.

For a couple of hours I sat slumped over my folded arms at a table, sleeping. When I awoke it was three o'clock in the morning and a group of broad-shouldered men were playing cards at the table next to mine. They paid no attention to me as I got up and put my leathers on. It was still raining and very dark. I loaded the bike with my saddlebags, wiped the seat dry, heaved the machine round in the puddles and gravel and set off again. On a journey like this, one badly-placed cow can slide you to your doom.

Alone in such extreme conditions, I felt secure on my bike. It was the instrument of mediation between me and whoever I should meet. The impact of first meetings with people in foreign lands cannot be underestimated, where not to be a trader might mean that you are an enemy. Away from this precious machine I felt lost. I almost did not exist. Yet aboard the machine I was also partly invisible. The interest from people by the road was not at first directed at me but at the bike; then they would notice the rider. This gave me time to adjust and negotiate a conversation.

Diary: South Eastern Bulgaria on the way to Istanbul
The project is suddenly in real jeopardy. My front tyre punctured 200 miles from Istanbul the night before I was scheduled to freight my bike to India. My lights had failed in the countryside at the base of the Bulgarian Alps but I foolishly continued. What else could I do - stay there and wait for help that might never come? And now I had a puncture. I was angry with myself as I stood cursing in the dark. I knelt down and bowed my visor to the surface of the road and roared and tempered. I cried, remonstrating with my life in the darkness. I cursed my lowly position in tears, face down against the asphalt. Just one kilometre from the sanctuary of a trouble-free hotel and there I was, stuck, with this scared rabbit in my head.

Somewhere before the Alps I rode hard into a hole in the road and both headlights went out. I should have stopped, but I decided to continue without front lights across high mountains in the middle of the night. It was still winter and snow piled up where the forest joined the black asphalt. After a while I became convinced that the front tyre had begun to deflate and I stopped to check the wheel. The tyre was hard. Ten minutes later, and less than a mile away from the town where I was intending to stay for the night, there was a sudden bang. Sparks scorched the darkness, my handlebars locked and I couldn't steer. The road was about to take me.

My heart erupted. I braced myself for a fall, but somehow I stayed upright. I braked very delicately and brought the bike to a standstill. The front tyre had blown off the rim. It looked ruined and I had no spare.

I was now in the far east of Bulgaria, near the Turkish border. I would have to find a bus to Istanbul, where I hoped the Triumph dealer would give me another wheel and fix the lights. I would lose a day. Everything had been arranged for the smooth completion of stage one and I had blown it. I had chanced too much, chanced my project, risked my life, all for an extra twelve miles with no headlights.

I had been on the bike for forty-six hours. Since Budapest I had slept for only three hours, and that was huddled on a bench in a restaurant. From there to Bulgaria I had only stopped the bike to fuel and piss. The Romanian countryside had been flooded with unseasonable rains, and throughout the night I had been riding around cows that had wandered from their fields to lie on the roads. Now I was kneeling by my front wheel. The rim was smashed and the tyre was completely separated from the wheel. I lay down on the road in despair, closed my eyes and slept.

When I awoke I saw a light in the distance. I got up, and for an hour or more pushed the bike towards it. The light turned into a gas station, and the attendant was locking up for the night. I asked him if he would store my bike until the morning. Another guy drove me to a hotel and said he would pick me up after breakfast, and help me try to get my wheel fixed. I booked a room and went to bed. In a fit of exasperation I banged my fists against my pillow and then, oily and stained with the sweat of the night, slept until there was a knock on the door.

Exactly as he had said he would, this unknown man drove me round the back streets of town to find someone who would inspect the damage. The tyre hadn't burst as I had first thought, but the rim was bashed back half a finger's length and was unusable. We needed canny inventiveness, and I was lucky enough to be able to inspire people to help me - perhaps it was the lure of making a little money, and why not? So I was driven here and there by this Bulgarian chap in his Skoda, looking for someone who could heat the rim of the wheel and hammer it back into shape.

The countryside was full of rustics wheeling scrap in their barrows and rag men shouting from house to house for iron and bits and pieces. Out in the country we found someone who knew an elderly gentleman who grew vines in his patch of land. Next to his house he had a workshop and, most importantly of all, he had oxyacetylene bottles. I never knew his name. He had a round ruddy face. I knew instinctively that he was a good man. He looked happy and kind.

The old man heated the rim and hit it with blows mighty enough to take off his hand if his swing should miss. For an hour he heated and hit, with just enough force to knock the wheel back into shape and reseat the tyre. In his garden, chickens cruised around for scraps and children had sand in their hair from rolling around with the puppies. I left for Istanbul, where I was to be met by the Triumph service people who had been in business since the start of the month.

4

Bombay: The lost bike

I am in Bombay. There is a problem. I run out of the hotel, jump into a cab, rush to the cargo terminal and run to the Emirates office. I am losing by the minute what small time I have gained in Europe. I do not know when I shall be able to book a freight flight from Dubai to Bombay, nor from Calcutta to Bangkok. If I am seriously delayed the record is not lost, but the timing of the rest of the journey will be tight and I will secure the record only by hours instead of days.

I am now in the Emirates office where assistant duty manager Sabu tells me that the bike is still in Dubai and has been held up because of improper packing. He tells me that this is the fault of his airline for not overseeing the process properly in Istanbul. While I accept that these mistakes happen, I am quietly in tears. Adventures soak up so much emotion and sometimes they stretch me so that I snap. After sixteen years of adventuring this is one of my greatest tests. I do not want to fail - even if I later have to ride day and night in Australia and America.

"*Why is this record so important to you?*"

"I don't know. I can't help myself. Something inside me won't let me stop."

"*Perhaps it's some psychological need which refuses to be fulfilled.*"

"Maybe I suffer from grey dogs in my head, classical morbidity, which I strive to overcome. Maybe I do it because I just want to do it."

"It's a curse."

"Yes, it is."

"No balance or moderation."

"Last night I dreamed of darkness. I was a small boy. I was alone. My Dad had gone. That small boy closed his eyes tightly and his body began to compact into a heaviness so huge that it collapsed under its own weight. He was suddenly smaller than a pin head and unable to move. His eyelids were heavier than the moon."

I could be on a beach now or at a hill station, or drifting down a river with my bike strapped in a pirogue to some dusty destination. Instead, I have to ride 1227 miles to reach Calcutta, weaving between potholes and crazy dogs. The near-misses with the trucks will raise my heartbeat to the point where my head feels as if it will explode. Then I will have to engage again in the same weary freighting process that nearly defeats me.

I want to take tea in the Fairlawn Hotel on Sudder Street, served by waiters with white gloves and red fezzes underneath fans and pictures of the Queen. Instead I am in a scruffy little room that is painted the sort of aquamarine blue you see in men's urinals. I am waiting for telephone calls from the relevant people - sponsors, freighters and PR people - to discuss what to do next. Failure looks possible. I feel sick about the possibility that the Guinness Book of Records might not accept the delay as part of the project. It is dusk now and my body is greased with hot sweat.

From the roof of my hotel I can see the length of the street and see traders spooning their wares into the pockets of passers by. There is a bird standing by a puddle, speaking to himself, his words singing in the wind. Nearby, a blade of grass sprouts out of the concrete and bows to him. The bird flies in a circle, touching the water with his wings and making silver ripples. This will be his suburban courtship. Far from home, the bird tries again and tells the blade of grass of things it has not seen; of the red Ibises that stand in long rows on the banks of the Nile and catch goldfish with their beaks; of the Sphinx, who is as old as the world and lives in a desert; of the beating of drums that echo across empty quarters; of the Mountains of the Moon and Air; of the people who live on floating islands in a lake high above the plains.

5

I read once that Bombay's population was around eight million people, of whom half live on the streets. I have recently been told that by the year 2050 it will have doubled. No-one really knows, because such an exponentially-expanding population from a migrant base of country people cannot be counted; and even if it could, who would want to, who would update it, and who would pay for the census? Bombay is one of the most densely-populated cities in the world, outstripped for humans-per-square-metre only by

Tokyo, New York and the city suburbs of Rio. Yet within the city, thick with auto rickshaws and taxis, trucks, buses, smiling faces and crimpelene trousers, no-one touches unless it is intended.

The words 'family planning' have been replaced in India by 'family welfare'. It is, as one local minister stated, "a euphemism for all that is wrong with population control". India's population is 945 million. It is the second most populous country in the world after China, whose population is 1,013 million. In the next 25 years China's growth will increase her population by 205 million while India will grow by 350 million. According to the latest estimates from the Census Commissioner, the population of India will, during the 21st century, reach 2 billion.

The computer that was the size of a room thirty years ago is now a small box on my knees. If artificial intelligence is to do with RAM size, the Random Access Memory in the hard drive of the computer, and if the human body is simply a bag of trillions of electrical connections, then it is only a matter of time before computers acquire enough RAM to perform all the electrical tasks that human bodies perform. Every thought is, in its simplest form, merely the passing of electrical impulses across synapses. RAM size is now doubling every two years and by the year 2050 there will be enough RAM available to imitate every electrical impulse in the human body. By that same year, it is said that human beings will have outstripped the resources available on this planet and will no longer be able to grow enough food to feed themselves. Computers don't need food.

6

Away from the crowds, sitting quietly on my bike, I look at the clouds; magnificent forms drifting across a blue sky; unimaginable castles of extraordinary light and beauty. The looking costs nothing and requires only quietness for watching and listening. Not even naming. Naming prevents the watching and we become a slave to the words. Without motive or zeal, you see and listen without distortion, and the noise of life is not chaos any more.

Being in India has hardened my thoughts, not because of the country's preordained spirituality but because of the technical exercises attached to it. There is devotion to the icon, the flickering light bulb against pictures of this or that god on a high shelf over a dusty shop doorway, but rarely does anyone talk of insight into self. The mechanics of making money complement a simple, trusting prostration before the deity, the priest, the politician, the logician. Words recited from childhood become clichés embalmed in a memory passed on from each generation to the next, but there is nothing in them of the mountains and the shadows, the tiger and the stream.

The paperwork for importing the bike into India is still being processed. If I have to wait here much longer I shall have to ride day and night in Australia and the States to claw back lost time. The tension makes me feel sick. To distract myself this painful bureaucracy I jump on a bus and then a train and then an autorickshaw, and save myself one pound. In local currency that's a full day's pay for the stone-breakers.

It is the highlight of a day otherwise occupied with paperwork and bickering custom officials.

All the next day I continued with the entry procedures for India. The freighters guided me from the airport to the docks, to the Indian Automobile Association and more faxes from their counterpart in England, back to the office of the freighters, back to the docks, and then to the airline company to help with the release of my bonded cargo at the airport. A final signature for the Municipal Corporation of Bombay Authority allowed me only 48 hours in the city before penalties could be invoked.

"You cannot go without a cup of tea," said the bondsman. "Come, drink chai with us before you go." And he immediately dispatched men to guard my bike while we exchanged convivialities. After chai I was allowed to go, straight on to the streets of India. It was teatime in Bombay. The dust in the street danced on beams of sunlight decaying in the thinning daylight as I raced off into the traffic.

I felt free on the bike. It was heavy but I rode it like a jockey on a horse. The similarity to the horse will always be there, and I am the machine-tickling aphid on its back.

That night in the dark in Bombay, a fault with the satellite-tracking system fused the charging unit that was connected to the bike's alternator, and disabled the radiator fan. This tracking device released a microwave emission for four seconds every hour to any passing satellite. This was monitored by my sponsors, and would form part of the presentation to the Guinness Book of Records as evidence of my journey's progress. Wires had short-circuited somewhere and the bike's lights were dimming in dense city traffic. I replaced two fuses, after which the charging began to function again, but only weakly. The water tank continued to boil over every ten miles. I had no choice but to ride back to my hotel and stay overnight again in Bombay.

The next day I set off before dawn. I was on the bike before the hawkers had set up their tables, before the night air had yet dissolved into morning and before the roads had become congested with the massive swill of people; so early that even Bombay rubbed its eyes to wake. Riding slowly through suburbs of concrete and ragged gardens, I began to follow the Ulhas River from Shahapur to Igatpuri past beautiful lakes and crammed cesspools. By noon I was winding up through the forested slopes of the Ghats, where the road was hot enough to bake bread and the pavements could have casseroled a stew.

The highway, routes three and six from Bombay via Narik towards Dhule and Nagpur, was too narrow for trucks to pass safely. Trucks were chasing each other at 100 metre intervals for as far as I could see. I was forced to ride at their speed - 30 miles every hour all day - in a shroud of blue-black diesel fumes. Overtaking was hazardous, but I managed to scrape between the sides of opposing trucks.

Before long the bike began to overheat again, a consequence of the radiator fan failing to operate. Twice an hour, water and steam spewed from underneath my seat and I was forced to stop and wait for the bike to cool. It seemed each time I did this that I had been waiting all day for the engine to cool. I checked the fuses and replaced them again, but I still had to wait in the sun by the side of the road.

To make a delicately balanced situation worse, in the critical period of acceleration between 32 and 37 miles per hour my front wheel had begun to lurch and wobble from side to side. The truth was that every few minutes I was riding on the edge of control. Three times I nearly crashed. The wobble wasn't caused by a broken fork seal; there was no oil and dirt leaking down the fork. Maybe the profile of the tyres had flattened. Speed on this stretch of road was critical - too fast and I was forced constantly to overtake, too slow and I was forever being overtaken. Somewhere inbetween I had to grip the reins tight. In my riding experience this was the second worst traffic environment I had encountered. Ecuador at night in the rain was the worst.

I rode all day and late into the night in the wind, around cows and brown Brahmins, emaciated and stringy. I rode round little boys who rushed in front of me, clearly unable to calculate my speed, eager to see a big red racing bike, wanting to have the hot machine smells spread over their faces from the fast-rushing air. They were shrieking; I was laughing. They ran after me shaking their hands, begging me to stop. The countryside whisked by in a blur of speed.

If there were to be any surprises here, they wouldn't be topographical. I had seen it before. Stumpy, drought-resistant shrubs lined the road, and ochre-coloured soil dipped into valleys browned on the edge of the Western Ghats. High on the Deccan Plateau, copper-coloured citadels of scrawny mountains gritted vertiginous teeth into a sky which presented little complexion, except as a backdrop for the thorny savannah; deep bottle-green set against sepia. It was like riding in one of the film society's old movies; 16mm reality crisping in the sun. Suddenly I felt I was dreaming. Or maybe not dreaming, but overwhelmed by a feeling of being other-worldly; so out of context that it was like being on a different planet.

I stopped to fill the radiator reservoir with water, and I was at a standstill once again somewhere in an Indian desert. When I asked the local people for water, a small man who stood as tall as the top of my leg brought over a can and then sent a boy on an errand to the well. I waited, standing in my leathers, as sweat began to run down my back. The boy had not yet returned with water and there I stood, soaking in my own body fluids.

7

"What is it that you search for when you go so far for so long?"

"The taste of death ahead of me."

"Don't you think that's a bit perverse?"

"Delicacies are fashioned best without dressing; to eat the comb of honey and drink the fresh ferment of coconut with an unrinsed mouth is as much as I can expect from life."

"You're talking in riddles. You're trying to do the Zen thing and to be honest I never understood the concept of the one-handed clap."

"Neither did I, but I do understand the difference between the mechanical and the artistic. There is something elegaic about pistons that behave like the poetic pieces of machinery the makers intended them to be. An engine that screams for mercy as you accelerate to the limiter. But what I don't understand is how three pistons collectively turn the crankshaft through 216 revolutions per second, 13,000 revolutions per minute, 780,000 per hour, or 14,040,000 every day."

8

If natural selection designed us for a lifetime of seasonal journeys through a blistering land of thorn-scrub or desert; if our instincts were forged in the desert; then it is easy to understand why greener pastures sometimes pall on us; why possessions haunt us; and why Pascal's imaginary man found his comfortable lodgings a prison. I was an imaginary man too, made real only fleetingly by a sea of faces gawping at me. On I blasted, edging across this little continent on the way to the other side of the world.

Eight hours later, I stopped that first night on the road to Calcutta in Bhusawal, a poor, small town that may never know better. For some people there will be progress and for others not. India may be trying to drag herself into the 20th century, but in towns such as this, the spittle and the betel juice squirted from the mouths of insouciant men still drips down the dirty white facades of buildings that line the small

34

town square. It is a curiosity that in the age of the gigabyte there are still whole towns that gob on the sidewalk.

In the desert of Rajasthan there is a city where the faces of all the people become pink in the evening sun. The walls of this city are pink, made with the pinkest stone hewn from the pinkest of lands. This is a small town where some people are clean and cherubic while others are dirty and covered in flies.

That evening, I had dinner there with several men, one of whom was a truck driver. They told me that 90% of truck drivers in India are HIV positive. It is a case of their brains being fastened to the loosening of their belts, their balls and cocks too indiscriminate. If pilots are the kings and train drivers the prince regents of public transport, then drivers of trucks and buses are the urchins, adept at catch-as-can, conniving to kill. They have a surly attitude to anyone else on the road and giving way to them is inviting death. I think there is a conspiracy between the truck drivers and the rocks: only rarely do they collide. Somehow scree is detonated down the mountain sides instead, to crash on to the road below. I am lucky to miss the rocks. Lucky to miss the grilles of the trucks.

That night I slept on a mattress on the floor of a local government official's rest house. I lay down feeling 300 years old and rose in the morning like a boy. After leaving Bhusawal I rode strongly throughout the second day across India to Nagpur, the midway point between Bombay and Calcutta and virtually the geographical centre of the country. I rode across the plains through Akola and into the city centre chaos of Amravati, where trucks and rickshaws beat a way through dense crowds of people in air made torrid by the violent heat. I felt faint. I was not cooling but I was still moving, and the record attempt, for what it was worth, was still on.

By late afternoon I had made it to Nagpur, and checked into a big smart hotel. The management let me drive my bike into the marble concourse by the fountain, underneath a large chandelier. The owner was a rich man who I never saw smile.

"I have driven from Bombay to Nagpur in seventeen hours and I am thinking that you are very slow in taking nearly twice the time," he said to me. I smiled at his greasy sarcasm but my heart sagged. I was tired, not because of having ridden 550 miles in the past thirty-two hours with only six hours rest, but because progress had been tense in almost the worst riding conditions imaginable. I had ridden fourteen hours each day and managed to average less than twenty-two miles per hour.

Speed, hesitation, confidence, complacency, angst, urgency and the brassy demeanour of a man sometimes out of sway accompanied me. I had expected more from myself but could give only what I had, only what the road would allow. I now looked less for the new in front of me and more for what I could leave behind that was not indispensable.

Walking to my room, I felt as clumsy as the fat plodding people in the corridor. I washed, watched Manchester United on TV, ate in the restaurant, chatted and slept. The next day I left Nagpur. I rode on to Durg and Raipur and into Orissa, the third poorest state in India.

Wherever I fuelled up in India I would see slops of oil

chucked down the nearest drain to slosh through the culverts below, along with the piss and pestilence. The oil runs slowly to the sea or finds its way back into the cracking mains, to the reservoir, the sewage works, standpipe, water carrier, kettle, and into cups of chai with two sugars, cinnamon and milk.

For most of my life I have felt my wealth within me, just in being alive...well, most of the time. I think that a source of wisdom is watered and renewed by vision gathered from springs of fresh wonders. The joys I need are there to be found at the roadside. But now on this journey I'm tired all the time, too tired to see; aching too much to smell the dust as it sifts around my face when I rest my cheeks against the hot earth and try to sleep for brief moments. You are the type of rider you are; gentleman-courier, or carrier of letters and parcels, or winged messenger, or gladiator, or warrior-poet, or racer who thrashes across the Milky Way.

The heat of the afternoon was from the Book of Revelations. It scorched me in my leathers with a crippling intensity. The zip burned against my sternum. I observed the winsome sallowness of the road-cleaners of Calcutta who shovelled up the turds of dogs and humans. They looked like brown bunches of string beans dried in the sun.

Diary: One of my favourite cities in the world, Calcutta
Have just arrived in Calcutta after one of the most gruelling motorcycle journeys I have ever experienced. The transport system across the country is the most maniacal I have seen anywhere. After twenty years of biking and after two major

biking expeditions, each of over 30,000 miles, I have never come so close to the edge.

Not that India is difficult in her nature - she is generous and benevolent if you know where to look and how to receive, but sometimes all there is to have is the heat.

9

It was a distance of 1267 miles from Bombay to Calcutta, and every few miles there were trucks bashed and scattered in bits. There was a head-on crash so recent that those who had survived it were sheltering in the shadows, chewing on their lunch as if this was how it was always meant to be. Two motorists lay dead, covered with a blanket, their feet sticking out, still wearing sandals.

The local policeman on the scene was more intrigued by my passing than by what he had to clear up. He was especially interested in the video camera fastened to the front of my bike. To him this scene was commonplace, but I had never seen a dead person before, not even bare legs not quite covered by a blanket. As the convoy of trucks filed past, weaving around the wreckage, I could see that up the hill the truck drivers were still battling for supremacy round blind corners in their joust with life. I rode for fourteen hours and arrived in Calcutta late in the afternoon.

I had set off at three in the morning from Sambalpur, and had ridden through the day to finish the last 100 miles straight to Calcutta, as perfectly diabolical in my riding style as the truck drivers. I was quite crazed, yet calm. I was at one with the bike and the heat, and felt every bump in the road. I was becoming like them. But today I was not meant to die. I had no need to worry about my fate. It still felt odd to be a fraction of a moment from oblivion; a heartbeat away from the closure of life.

Whenever I stopped anywhere for tea I was immediately surrounded by a group of villagers, maybe a 100 or more. The only cheap privacy in India was in sleeping and shitting, and both followed dawn before breakfast. All these things were of my own choice, and I was condemned to the kind of freedom where I had nothing left to lose. Not achieving journeys like this would be for me like not really living. It would be like existing in some half world, never having drunk enough of the heroism of life.

Sometimes as I rode there were spectres in my daydreams which made me feel as if I had left my body; stained glass images forming in my head as I sat on the bike like an automaton. And there were the echoing sounds of a small boy running down the alleyways of my past. Instead of seeing oncoming trucks in the dust and the savannah shrub, I seemed sometimes to be looking down from a promontory overlooking the sea, held back from falling by a tall man in a long coat. And in my mind I pictured a bridge of iron that reached across the waves, and I knew that if I tried to walk across the bridge it would turn to air. It was the narcosis of having too many thoughts locked in my helmet for too long.

Often when I stopped I would be bruised by the crowds pressing up against me. I would sit quietly on my bike until the jostling started a slight panic in my helmet; then I would suck and blow like a baby, my breath steaming up the inside of the visor. I would smell the sweat of half the town and see the brittle smiles of poverty, virtuous only because it is easier to share nothing than it is to share plenty. In these parts charity is cold in a multitude of possessions and the rich are covetous of their crumbs.

I felt they sensed my shallow lungs and breathing, far away from home, and always I was offered time to climb off the bike and rest in the arms of some hut man serving chai on the side of the road. I would sit awkwardly, moistened with sweat. In a dark storeroom of leather, my testicles became the size of stones in avocado pears and took on the bitter-sweet smell of a swamp.

I listened. Everything was in the voices. As I sat drinking chai I thanked them humbly. In one place I had been brought in from the road, away from the village, to be seated on a bench. The hut had mud walls hardened by the heat, and smelt of cinnamon and drying clay. The old man whose chai hut this was had a grey beard, and eyes that seemed to enjoy his small public relations coup. In fits and starts of novelty he bade people come to meet me, only to scatter them back on to the street.

There were marketers nosing through the doorway, but they always gave the game away. Eyebrows would twitch as they glanced around the bike, ready to seize the chance to make a killing. Their breathing would change, charged through a dry throat.

"Nice bike, tell me, how much?"

"No idea, it was given to me by my sponsors," I would say. "Goodness knows I couldn't afford it myself."

"Ah yes," they would murmur, placated by the fact I was not as rich as I seemed.

Villagers understood well the concept of the bike. It was sleek and powerful, like a stallion. With the butch charisma of a stallion's mate I was one with it as we slowed and stopped for chai. It would take an Indian on an average salary ten years to buy such a machine if he saved every rupee he earned. Then he too would be able to race up to sixty miles per hour in three-and-a-bit seconds, and for a moment be faster than a MIG fighter at take-off. To people who lived on clay floors it was like a space ship; a time machine that transported people to and from futuristic places of which these villagers knew nothing. The satellite tracking device was understood to be somehow like the Star Television that beamed down from the troposphere to the village set. Around all this was their perception of a man no different to them who was racing across their country. "India the great", we shouted together, enforcing a perception passed on by the propaganda of hope and political invective that starves its people. Of tales of real people's life savings put into imaginary investments in imaginary cattle and imaginary crops.

People here didn't travel much, and in the smaller pockets of village life the only women around were from neighbouring

41

collectives, first or second cousins, or just plain silly. Children occasionally ran to me, some of them harebrained with unearthly features, calm only when they slept or shat. In some of the villages in the jungle their heads hung lopsidedly. If you gently coaxed a little child to press the electric start of the bike and create a roar of engine noise, the village would cheer at the connection. It will take many times the length of my journey for this story to be told over the years to grandchildren of the village, but it will be the bravery of the boy in the crowd that I will remember, and the magician within me that was always there to smooth a frown into a smile.

So close to Calcutta, I still felt India in the raw. Dust from the road was under my fingernails. The road from Bombay to Nasik, less than a tenth of the total distance to Calcutta, was nightmarish. The dead people I had seen by the side of the road often came to my mind. The barrenness of Maharastra was made all the more stark by the gruff, sharp, foreboding mountains that rose from the semi-arid plain like shark teeth. If this were Australia, it would be an Aboriginal dream - the giant sharks across the desert that bite into the sky. The air pulsating in the heat gave the impression that the mountains were breathing. The heat baked dust into the wrinkles that had gathered on my face.

All day I rode, surrounded by forests of slender, shiny ashok, quivering pipal and the strangle-hold of banyan by the side of the road. The menthol scent of eucalyptus was widespread at the edge of villages and filtered through my visor. I slowed past lines of schoolchildren in crisply clean white shirts and navy blue shorts and skirts. The bike sounded strong. Its individual components meshed with each other, composing their own mechanical symphony, slipping in a thin covering of oil.

In front of me now as I rode was a valley full of flowering trees. Purple-blue jacarandas nestled against clusters of the red and yellow flowers of tamarind, handsome with its short straight trunk and large spreading crown. I liked the trees that lined the roadside because they were now my only view of India and I peered through the scarlet flowers of tulip and coral trees, the light green gul mohurs feathered out like peacocks, as I wound around the empty hilly lanes that ultimately would drop towards the plains far away. Dotted about were scenes of activity, of people carrying or hoeing. A journey like this demonstrates the reincarnation of the watcher and the watched. These scenes have been witnessed over and over again all through history.

Lower down the slopes before the plains, I rode through denser groves of mango and warty brown jackfruit. Tatty banana leaves were everywhere. Always I was passing by, rarely able to stop except for fuel or a quick feed. Peacocks scattered out of the way and rose-ringed parakeets screeched overhead. Alongside stretches of water there were cranes and storks. From the corner of my eye I saw a little kingfisher flash turquoise, making a rapid reflection of herself in the water.

Here in the backyard of India, delightful Orissa, I imagined bandits stalking me invisibly in the trees. I had the road to myself. I saw Indians walking their cattle from fields of finger millet and sorghum, tapioca and tea. Soon I was away from the hills and along the plains of West Bengal. Villages became towns, and the quiet had been replaced by the hum and clatter of masses of people and honking horns and bicycle bells. I swooped like a swallow past slow-moving Ambassador cars, overtaking everything. Cloaked by the invisibility of fast movement, I passed unobserved, braking only for the dogs and children who ran from behind trees and the corners of houses.

When I was a child I wrote a poem, a Japanese haiku:

> *'Surrounded by friends*
> *I look around*
> *And find that I am all alone.'*

Here, I looked around and found that I was alone. Good. No cars, no bullock carts, no animals on the road, no people nor policemen. I went like a fury through the forests and the trees. Faster and faster in a breathtaking burst of speed that turned the road into a tunnel of wood. Then with my heart racing to burst, I slowed and settled into the rhythm of the day.

10

For hours and hours every day I thrust this machine forward. I ride all day and sometimes all night. And always there are thoughts in my head fighting for space. If nature abhors a vacuum, so does my head.

"But you travel so fast, what can you see? Surely you just go past everything so quickly that you see nothing."

"I do see, I see in my head the emporiums, the high-sided buildings, buffed and fluted columns, monoliths of glass."

"In Calcutta?"

"I see the towns and villages, washing hanging from mossy balconies made murky by the fumes of traffic. I see the drains, and boys and girls washing in the ponds with the oxen, old men in dhotis carrying black umbrellas to transport their shade."

"But there are no monoliths of glass here, just the new bridge over the Howrah, the dilapidated Wills factory as you come off the bridge, the potholes on Chowringhee, the usual freaks around Sudder Street by the museum, the armless people and the necrotics who lie in their own shit and sores. What is this beautiful place you describe?"

"It's an imaginary place, all the images I have seen juxtaposed into one. Snatches of things, moments crushed in a vacuum."

"You know what I mean. That isn't real, it's not even the journey you're describing. It's like something you want to describe which bears no relationship to what you actually see and what you should be describing. How can it be real if you describe your journey in such absurd terms?"

"It's not absurd. Thoughts and opinions, like the borders that line every road, complement each other in opposite directions. Think of all the great sages, who in their silence, have soaked up erudition and harmonised laws of all things."

"You're being imaginary again... "

"No I'm not. Marco Polo would have stood on the outskirts of Qilian Shan or Sinklang and faced the forces of the wind and the sand. Anyone who has stood flanked by a horizon of hairless hills and trees would feel the same."

*"But this is not what you **should** be describing."*

Should had nothing to do with it. What did people in my home town think of where I went and what I did? To them it would not be real but no-one had suggested to me that my journeys were absurd. What was Timbuktu to them, or the salt caravans from Taoudenni, or the red road from Bujumbura, or the pink rooms on the island of Amantani smelling of coca and lime, or the people who transported shadows in wheelbarrows? It was absurd to me that everyone didn't motorbike around the world. What was it that strapped them to their mortgages? Why couldn't they leave the housing estates and factories?

The rattling I heard in my head would not stop. It was the accumulation of years of other people shaking their heads. They say that I'm a nice bloke, but a bit of a nutter.

"If you see a plant in a window that needs watering, you must first break the glass. Depending on your view, this is a Zen thing and is okay, or is the action of a disturbed individual. Take your pick."

"But I'm not a disturbed individual. I'm just like you. It's not what you think. I have the same mortality, same fears, same needs, frustrations. I cry in the night like you all, cursing my demons, expressing my love."

"You see, you are a nutter. YOU ARE A NUTTER."

"No I'm not."

"You speak in poetry. You break windows to water a flower. You speak as if you don't want to be understood."

"So you're telling me that the totems of modernity I see everywhere beside the cathedrals and the palaces can't mingle with the fragrance of franipangi from open grassy places?"

"Beautiful buildings might smell sweetly, but what is the point in trying to convey an irrelevance? This journey isn't about Corinthian pillars and fluted columns, it's about the hardness of a journey, the speed of a machine, the pushing of frontiers and, let's face it, the suffering."

Perhaps the reflection in my helmet needed a reality check on the hour along with the news. In the distance, sepia-coloured hills were shimmering, calling to me to carry on. The brownness only added to the effect of formidable wilderness that India can become, away from the road. Close by, Flame trees stood motionless in a dead wind. Against my fingertips the thin metal of my petrol tank had begun to burn. The stillness of a journey in the heat of the day makes everything glow. Now there were three conversations in my head. I felt myself fragmenting.

"I know about bad situations. I know about concrete alleyways as places for beatings and pissings and the stench of vomit. I see the looks from evil men who would torture me for my magnificent bike. In my world, if you show fear you will find it. What you give off, your attitude, the vibrations of

47

your soul, the widening of an iris, can shape the day with wonder or horror. This is what men looking for fear see."

"I'm not sure that we understand each other."

"If you look for these things, you will find them. But if you are not aware of them, you will pass unmolested."

"I disagree. What you describe is an exercise in fine thinking that bears no relationship to real life for ordinary people. If you carry on like this, people will think you really are mad."

"What should adventure be? If you want simply the annunciation of bravery then you must find those who travel in the courageous lands of yore; the angry lands, the crazy lands; mad, high, hot, cold, vast, wide and unspeakably horrid lands."

I wondered at how real these conversations had become. It seemed to me that alter ego, or dream thought, was another way of energy meeting energy across dimensions, a meeting of two minds simultaneously apart and together.

"I have a right to say these things because it is me who is here and me who is there. It is me who has been to all of these lands on this red bike that breathes like a stallion with its pistons and machinery, its tappets tapping and the rhythm of an engine in balance. Although I cannot deny that sometimes in the brooding light, I would rather set sail in the blue sky than roar like a lion across the plain."

The conversations in my head exhausted me. I knelt down beside my bike and slept for four hours. When I woke, mist was swirling around the forest. A *crie du chat* sounded from

"It is the clockmaker's pendulum. The earth is a bob, where each oscillation of history is repeated again and again and bounced off the moon."

"Off the moon?!"

"The earth is tossed by the sun. It is the circus act of this collosal mechanism. It is the epoch of the ages and it happens every day."

There was no sound from the engine now and I became aware of how quiet this journey could be. Serenity comes in small moments of contemplation. Everyone needs to go where they will not be disturbed, yet by simply being, they were already there. It is the great irony of rides like this that the engine both takes you to and separates you from that quiet place of reason.

The barrenness of Maharastra was made all the more stark by the gruff, sharp, foreboding mountains that rose from the semi-arid plain like shark teeth. If this were Australia, it would be an Aboriginal dream - the giant sharks across the desert that bite into the sky. The air pulsating in the heat gave the impression that the mountains were breathing. The heat baked dust into the wrinkles that had gathered on my face.

If natural selection designed us for a lifetime of seasonal journeys through a blistering land of thorn-scrub or desert; if our instincts were forged in the desert; then it is easy to understand why greener pastures sometimes pall on us; why possessions haunt us; and why Pascal's imaginary man found his comfortable lodgings a prison.

Far from home, the bird tries again and tells the blade of grass of things it has not seen; of the red Ibises that stand in long rows on the banks of the Nile and catch goldfish with their beaks; of the Sphinx, who is as old as the world and lives in a desert; of the beating of drums that echo across empty quarters; of the Mountains of the Moon and Air; of the people who live on floating islands in a lake high above the plains.

Last night I dreamed of darkness. I was a small boy. I was alone. My Dad had gone. That small boy closed his eyes tightly and his body began to compact into a heaviness so huge that it collapsed under its own weight. He was suddenly smaller than a pin head and unable to move.

His eyelids were heavier than the moon.

Desert heat had the trick of making clocks stand still for travellers.

During the day the sharpness of the horizon was diluted by the shimmering air, and the will to voyage was diminished by the coolness of the shadows.

Everywhere was brown. Brown mountains and brown trees, brown people with sandy-coloured dogs, and a brownness in the baked air.

Alexander said in 326 BC: *"This ocean is connected with the Myrcanian Sea for the great Stream of Ocean encircles the earth. Moreover I shall prove to you, my friends, that the Indian and Persian Gulfs and Myracanian seas are all three connected and continuous. Our ships will sail round from the Persian Gulf to Libya as far as the Pillars of Hercules, whence all Libya to the eastwards will soon be ours, and all Asia too, and to this empire there will be no boundaries, but what God himself has made from the whole world."* He invited comments from the officers present and only after a long silence did Coenus, son of Polemocrates, pluck enough courage to speak. *"Sir, if there is one thing above all others a man like you should know, it is when to stop."*

the tops of the trees. It was a sound that could have been clawed from the soul.

11

I thought about my disastrous night-time ride without lights in Bulgaria, when I had wrecked my front wheel because I had tried to gain an extra twelve miles. I had cost me half a day's journey and had forced a series of events that had cost me a day in Istanbul. Perhaps because the freighters and I rushed the packing, we were delayed in Dubai for two days. It was due to this delay that we were held up in Bombay, because one of the clearing days fell on a local state holiday. Then, because of this, I was late leaving Bombay and late arriving in Calcutta, and so missed my flight to Bangkok and had to wait another day. Now I have just found out that I am to arrive in Bangkok on the one weekend of the year when customs are closed. Is there something being said to me that I do not hear?

12

The poorest state in India is Bihar - a state to be avoided at all costs at night. I have travelled through it by train, but it is getting increasingly desperate. Half the state's 1,156 police stations have no vehicle. Only 400 stations have telephones, of which 50% are disconnected because the bills have not

49

been paid. 450 stations are simply thatched huts without lockup facilities. Sixteen people are either killed, robbed or kidnapped every day.

And then there's the matter of rubbish in Calcutta. As a result of India's economic reforms and increased prosperity, in the past decade garbage has been produced at twice the rate of population growth. Only eight of India's 3,119 towns and cities have full wastewater and treatment facilities; another 209 have partial facilities; the rest have none at all. In Calcutta, 27% of the 6,800 tonnes of garbage generated every day remains uncleared.

A third of India's urban population has no access to sanitation facilities. It is worse in the smaller towns. In Lucknow, 70% of the population sends its wastes into the Gomti river. In Gulbarga, Karnataka, 87% of the population isn't connected to a sewage system. Indian cities generate around 80,000 tonnes of garbage every day. That is enough to fill up trucks heaped with garbage and lined bumper-to-bumper for 180 miles - the distance from Delhi to Jaipur. Some 300,000 children die every year because of dysentery linked to unattended waste. In Bombay, where there is a sewage system that was laid down by far-sighted British planners who were building in a time when the city was just a string of fishing villages, 93% of the untreated sewage now goes directly into the sea, killing all marine life along Bombay's coast. 40% of Delhi's sewage is untreated. In most Indian cities, water pipelines run alongside sewers. Slum-dwelling families of five people produce 0.5 kilograms of trash per day and while it is estimated that similarly sized upper-class families produce ten times this amount.

In the three centuries of its history, Calcutta has grown from a fishing village into the largest city in India, with a population of 12 million. (Some say 80 million). It is one of the largest cities in the world. Calcutta served as the capital of British India until 1912 and western architecture, mostly Victorian is the predominant style. There are 600 red London-style double-decker buses in the city, but only 150 work at any one time; the rest are being repaired because of overloading. The average number of passengers aboard a London bus at any given time is 17; in Calcutta it is 73. Before the new bridge was built there was only one bridge connecting the north and south sides of the city. One bridge to serve 12 million people. In London there are 16 bridges serving 8 million people. It is said that at five in the afternoon, when the office workers tramp across the bridge to get to their homes, the combined fall of their feet makes the bridge resonate, and if everyone walked in unison it would collapse.

13

In Calcutta I stayed at the Fairlawn Hotel, owned and run by Violet and Ted Smith. Ted was archetypal stiff upper lip English, parting down the lower left cranial, teetering around his upper seventies. Violet, all lipstick and pencilled-in eyebrows, was his Armenian wife, part of the Raffles Hotel dynasty. She wafted around the hotel with a turquoise rinse and poodle to match, dispensing sponge fingers to the clinking of her pearls and brooches.

Ted and Violet invited me for drinks in their private quarters, along with the head of customs from the British High Commission in Delhi and his counterpart out from England, who was on the trail of smugglers at source. We small-talked as the waiters in turbans and cummerbunds poured out gin and tonics. An electric storm gathered. Rain fell in large droplets, waving around the mussaenda and hibiscus, and sheet lightning played with the flowers of 'Lady of the Night'.

I knocked back three large ones and all the cashews nuts and suddenly stopped, remembering what I was doing.

"You know," said the customs official, "we will never curb the trade, what with people addicted to tobacco and alcohol and the fact that more people use antidepressants than marijuana." He sipped his gin. "It's all a bit pointless, you know."

"It's that word again," I said.

"It seems to me that the world's full of drug addicts," Ted said. "Sorry old boy, what was that?"

"That word."

"What word?"

"Pointless. You're right, it is all pointless."

"I suppose it is," said Ted, not sure what I was talking about. He decided to humour me with another gin and waved to one of his servants. "Ice and lemon, refresh it up a bit. Anyone else for a top-up?"

"You see, Ted, my girlfriend back in England wants to take me to a sperm bank, in case I fall off my bike."

Ted was suddenly silent and then guffawed into his drink. "Jolly good thing too, I should say," he said looking around. "Damn hazardous things these motorbikes, at the best of times."

"But it makes me sort of pointless, don't you see. Wank into a teacup in a cubicle, force-fed with a stack of men's magazines, it just doesn't make any sense to me. Best thing she could do would be to start over again, get a new bloke and start her life again. What do you think?" There was a silence.

"...Erm...I'm sure I don't know old chap," he said, looking around at his guests, who were by now so pissed that they didn't give a flying fart about anything as long as Ted kept on with the top-ups.

"What's he say?" Violet poked in for a quick nosey.

"I, erm, think his wife is off with another chap or something."

"No Ted," I said. "She just wants to save a bit of me for in-vitro fertilisation in case I fall off my bike."

"In what?" enquired Violet, trying to squeeze out a bit of gossip.

"Cashew nuts anyone?" murmured Ted.

If I had known how hard this journey was going to be, I would have stayed at home. Yet it wasn't really so hard. It wasn't misery. Misery is having a rotting finger from which maggots are being pulled by tweezers without sedation. (Surely the maggots should be given something to relieve the pain?)

Yesterday I visited Mother Theresa's hospice for the dying in Kalikat, a couple of miles from the centre of Calcutta. My bike was being processed by customs so I had some spare time. The hospice was clean and the sisters went about their duties efficiently and cheerfully. Most of the people there will be cleaned up before being sent back on to the streets, before ending up back at the hospice for more treatment.

I thought one old man I saw would not survive. His finger looked as if it had been charcoal-burned and was crawling with maggots and although the maggots, were cleaning the wound, eating only dead tissue, it was hard to watch his suffering. Here was a cluster of grotesques, of leaky bladders and rectums unable to contain their slush, of necrotic fingers.

All over India villagers club together and put sick people on the train. They load them into the guard's van, where they lie until they reach Calcutta. Here the Sisters of Mercy pick them up from the platform and take them to Kalikat. In the words of a song I heard on the radio, *'It's hard to love a man whose legs are bent and paralysed.'* I think this is also misery.

Diary: Bangkok to Singapore
It's two in the afternoon and I'm waiting for the final details of the freighting so that the bike can be released. To help this process, boys run breathlessly from office to office with sheaves of papers held in brown card folders. A friend, Rangsi, is still with me. He is the assistant to a wonderfully mysterious unseen coordinator known only as The Captain. With his help the schedule is still holding, and we are due to meet a cameraman later in the afternoon at the Airport Hotel. The project is being documented at various points by film crews as well as by me. 21 countries, 21 cultures, nearly 20,000 miles, 31 days and a million forgotten faces. Out of one airport hotel and into another. Packing, repacking bags, remobilizing the bike, rewiring the battery, refuelling, pumping up the tyres, psyching myself up for another all-night ride. I know the route. I've cycled down it twice and driven along it on a motorbike once before. The hardest part will be the stretch down to the Thai-Malay border. Then the road turns into a three-lane motorway all the way to Singapore. At Singapore the first three stages of the project will have been completed. Europe, India and the Malay Peninsula done; Australia and New Zealand, the States and Europe still to go.

The freight handler ran around from office to office while I typed my story. The paperwork eventually came back to me processed and signed, and we went into the bonded warehouse to retrieve the bike. I saw that an indicator was broken and the front wheel rim was dented, though it was nothing that I hadn't ridden on before. I reconnected the battery, had just enough petrol to start the engine and rode slowly to the airport garage a couple of miles away. I pumped up the tyres, filled up the radiator reservoir under the seat, refuelled and filtered on to the main airport carriageway to Bangkok. A film crew trailed behind me and cars hemmed me in on all sides. Sometimes, when the surge of traffic closes in, the noise of a beating heart can fill the head with fear.

On corporate forecourts across Bangkok, trees dripped beguilingly with lights. Atriums of glass and steel reached the sky. Artefacts of architectural egoism dominated the skyline with a vanity that was absent in the countryside. I imagined that at the tops of these towers all the workers would be sitting in the clouds.

I saw little of the city, and nothing of the tops of the tall skyscrapers, from where they say you can see castles. There was a large temple beautifully adorned with gold leaf near the King's palace, but I was in a rush and couldn't stop to look. I sped quickly over the river and on to the road heading south. Rangsi unnecessarily led the way in his car and kept waving me to follow. All the way to Petchiburi, about 100 miles. He drove furiously and I had to keep up. It was hard frantic riding; it reminded me of riding in Equador in the dark on the busy Pan-Americana.

I left him after that and rode a further 60 miles to Hua Hin, where I stopped to stay for a couple of hours with an old friend. It was already two in the morning and I could sleep only until five. Of course I overslept. I left at six-thirty for the ride to Singapore, during which, apart from a rest on a bench north of Kuala Lumpur and obligatory fuel stops, my feet didn't touch the ground.

Thailand's roads after Hua Hin changed from dual to single carriageway, so to overtake trucks I had to flick the bike out, around, and then in front very rapidly to avoid colliding head-on with anything coming the other way. The time it took to gasp was all the time it would have taken to get it wrong. I rode hard past Prachuap Khiri Khan and into the next 111 miles to Chumphon.

I stopped for cold drinks in a midday temperature of 42 degrees centigrade. I had to soak my shirt in water and allow it to radiate my body heat as it evaporated before I could continue. In my leathers and helmet I was now unbearably hot. On the move, decisions were made under a blue cloudless sky, but the demonic whiteness of the sun was fiercely unforgiving when I stood beside the bike.

I rode on, stopping only for fuel. On to Surat Thani and Thung Song, 1250 miles since late night Monday, all day and all night Tuesday. Then on past Phatthalung, Hat Yai, Sadao to the Thai-Malay border which never closed.

Past midnight, a full moon in the sky, I rode into the Thai border customs and emigration area. Smart Thai officials in braids and tunics looked through my passport politely and quickly allowed me to pass. The coolness of the night calmed my aching body and I felt alert. Customs and entry procedures at the Malaysian border were equally efficient and quick, and I was informed that the road through Malaysia

57

was a super-highway, all the way to Singapore. This was good news. No potholes to fall into, no dogs to slide on. No bumps or sharp stones, just the smooth surface my bike deserved. As soon as I got into Malaysia I was on some of the best roads in the world.

It was the middle of the second night and I was still seeing only the ghostly outline of the view that lined the roadside. How could I say I had seen Malaysia when I passed through so much of it at night? Even in the early hours, 150 miles north of Kuala Lumpur between Taiping and during the long descent to Ipoh, I could only picture the topography from memory.

Later there was a storm. Towering flashes of lightning lit and shadowed gigantic plugs of tree-covered rock, making them stand out like sentinels for the gods of the jungle that embraced the winding highway. In between the geological rifts, deep in the jungle, in the old days of gin and Jaguar settlers, the tea-planters and vegetable farmers would have hauled their way up these mountain roads. In these places Hawk eagles and Brahminy kites soared from rift to rift. Crested Firebacks and Racquet-tailed Drongoes with sweeping tails stood next to saffron-coloured Orioles. Wagtails flitted and Mynahs stood with the hoarsely-coughing flower-peckers. Weaver birds hung from their tubular nests. During the day Monitor lizards basked on the hard shoulder and at night frogs belched for king and country. In the jungle there is never silence, but neither is there in the desert, where scarab beetles can be heard scratching over the sand. When you listen.

I stopped to sleep on a concrete bench in a rest area beside the motorway. Away from the bike, the smells were those of damp trees drying. It was like a steam room. Next to the bike, the air was hot with the smell of engine oil and the vapour from greasy components. I phoned Henrietta in England on my mobile phone and we chatted, and by the time we had finished I was covered in sweat. A cloud of love signs was needed to neutralise her angst, because I wasn't there with her to stroke away her dread. If only someone had explained to me that there are worse things than loneliness. That there are times you hear sounds so quiet they could easily not be there.

"Come home to me, hurry back for me," said the princess to the frog. "I need you more than all the stars in the night. Please don't make me live my life alone."

I pumped my jumper into a pillow and closed my eyes. Around me the leaves on the trees in the jungle waved sinuously. The sooner I fell asleep, the longer it would be before I had to wake. My thoughts became a dream of myself as a child, trapped on the edge of an endless sea, under a sky blacker than the deepest night. I wanted so much to be pleased to be myself, to be able to be the boy I had never been. Throughout my life, whenever things have become tedious, I have hypnotised myself with stories of travellers and kings and of cities beyond the mirages, where skies as yellow as saffron hold up a tryst of orange moons.

"So why do you do it? Is it so hard a question to answer?"

"To flee the ways of normality."

"And what is normal?"

"I don't want to get into that. You know what I mean. Anyway, motorbiking around the world is not a normal thing for most people to do, even though when you do it it's not abnormal."

"So?"

"Let's just say my mind needs to hunt alone in the wilderness."

"Oh really! That sounds rather expansive. I mean is the wilderness so hard to be in?"

"It's about angels sitting up high looking down. It's the wilderness of death I seek. Not to die, but to know about nearly dying, about crossing the divide and not being afraid when it happens."

"You talk about angels perching on the cliffs - well let's be real. I'm your angel and I'm sitting on your shoulder."

"Okay, okay. I trust in your annoying pragmatism. Everyone said how hard this journey would be and it's true it's not easy. But journeys like these teach you to endure simple anxieties which otherwise would be unendurable. One minute you're up and the next minute you're down. Peaks of euphoria followed by gulfs of despair. How can you really know unless you've done it?"

"That's just the way it is. Anyway, there are many things more unendurable."

"True, but unlike everyday life, adventures constantly involve life and death decisions. Several times each day I could easily be killed. Indian trucks, a pothole in the road at night, bandits targeting a lone foreigner. Death is death however it happens. There are times when you really need to be invisible. When a jungle yields its forms, a village turns into mist and a lake becomes a mirage. Solid things dissolve and things and people are not what they seem."

"It seems to me that you safeguard yourself with your own fairy tales. This is not the journey that happened, it is a make-believe one in your head. The more I listen to you, the more I think your feet stand in an abyss and your head radiates in empty spaces."

There was a breeze forming, I could feel it around my nostrils. In the distance a barking deer. I heard in the trees all manner of life ululating. My sleep was fed by the sounds of gentle presences. Tired from having ridden day and night, I no longer knew whether I was sleeping or not. My days were not always dramatic but my nights were as vivid as rainbows.

I slept that night in the wings of the closed-canopy forest, concealed by light and shade. The light thrown from what was left of the full moon gave me camouflage. I lay next to my bike in the starkly-contrasting black and white light. I saw, but was not seen by, passing tapirs, their light-brown spotted fur simulating the effect of sun-dappled leaf litter.

There was never enough time to talk to local people, so sometimes I would phone England and speak to a friend in some far-distant village or town. All this journeying around the world still left my telephone life intact. Only the sound of the night life in the background gave the game away.

I was on the road to Kuala Lumpur but I didn't know exactly where. I had no map. I don't always use maps. The deceptive flatness of the page with different colours for hills and plains creates an unreal sort of mental journey. One reality is linear and flat and full of the smell of burning candles and routes plotted from here to there. The other reality is the dusty road that escapes from the page and turns into palm trees that swing in the wind and seas that pound the shore. When I looked at the map of South America, the route for Peru seemed to run straight across the desert like the Nazca lines on roads as spindly as spiders' legs. The reality was quite different, and for hundreds of miles there were bends on cliff edges that teetered over crashing seas. I began to think that the scale of maps was too small to show all the details, but then my journeys were as big as the world and I needed a roomful of charts to trace every twist and turn.

I woke, got on my bike and rode for ten hours. Neither glance nor reflection passed between us as I skimmed Kuala Lumpur at lunchtime. Its big-windowed buildings were too busy presiding over their own vanities to look at me and I was in too much of a hurry to look at them. South of the city, jungle hills were replaced by plains, heath forest and lowland hill. Large expanses had been cleared by shifting cultivators who had created treeless swathes through the rain forest. Where primary forest had been logged to make way for secondary growth, coarse elephant grass swayed in the wind.

It was easy riding to the border of Malaysia and Singapore. The bike purred. It was my stallion, my battle machine. We slipped through the exit and entry procedures in a few minutes. Another film crew met me by the causeway and filmed until the later part of the afternoon. In between the shoots, I spoke to my travel people in England to sort out the final freighting schedule at the airport. I also squeezed in a press conference with Mobil, and all the national media turned up. It was a red carpet occasion and I enjoyed the attention.

The bike was to be flown out the following morning on the nine forty-five flight with British Airways and I was booked on a Singapore Airlines flight at about the same time. That night I checked into the Meridian hotel near the airport. I filled the bath to the brim and used all the soaps and salts, then ran around my room and jumped on the bed, pretending it was a trampoline. I was asleep within minutes.

I dreamed of my Dad passing away to another land. Only once before had I had a dream like this. It happened in Uganda in 1983 when I was cycling to the source of the White Nile and stayed overnight in a monk's cell in the jungle. In England my mum was taking her final breaths. I wrote in my diary:

Gulu - There was a stroboscope effect of flickering lights panning across the sky as if the intensity of the flash raised the tempo of the rain, the drum-beat on the corrugated roof. The rain dribbled from the corrugations, appearing motionless in the shivering light. A spider hung on grimly, swinging slightly. It wouldn't be there long. This was a spider-demolishing storm. The flashes of lightning made the mosquito netting look like the lines on a television screen, a

cathode-ray tube view of an electric storm. In the
distance was an empty field, the only space free from
foliage. In the near distance, with the emptiness behind,
a tree raised two arms and I saw a woman hanging. I
beckoned her to come to me, to umbrella her way
through the rain, to tell me it was not her hanging in the
tree, arms outstretched.

At the moment that her image appeared in my head I knew she was gone. She had sashayed across to some parallel universe and had come to say goodbye. It is said that loud prayer is good for weak lungs, but all I had was angels perched on the cliffs and the taste of grief in the shadows. They also say, the little spirits, that man is such a hive of parasites that it is doubtful whether his body is more theirs than his.

In my dream in Singapore there was an old blond-haired man and a willowy young girl, and there was a boat in a lock that looked like a dhow, except that it was huge. It was an odd-looking craft with high sails, and with back and front ends shaped like the apex of a wave. I had not yet worked out how to sail her, and she was so big that from the stern I could not see the bow. I didn't know if it was a pirate boat or one that would take me across a wide ocean. There were colours and parts of the whole that didn't make sense.

Then suddenly a horn hooted to set sail and I shot upright. My God, I had overslept. I looked at the clock. It was eight twenty-one and my flight to Perth left in an hour. I packed, raced out of my room, checked out, jumped in a cab and rushed to the airport. I exchanged my ticket reservation note for a ticket, checked in and raced to the gate with ten minutes to spare. Boarding was closed but they let me in, because my dream was still written across my face, and whatever was going to happen was not allowed not to.

16

Diary: Perth

Just arrived in Australia on the Singapore Airlines flight. Of the plane-load of people who disembarked, I was the only person Customs decided to check. "Oh do excuse me officer, come to think of it my bag does feel about sixteen kilos heavier than usual and no, I didn't pack it myself but allowed a very plausible young man from Afghanistan to help me. How may I be of assistance?" When I entered the arrival lounge a film crew turned on their lights. I thought that someone well-known was being greeted until I realised that it was for me. You start off being unknown and you end up becoming obscure, so I enjoyed another brief moment of fame.

The Triumph dealership at Perth is called JC's and is owned by John Slehofer. Bill was in spare parts and Derick was his mechanic. They were keen to sort the bike out because they said this sort of thing just didn't happen every day. They cared about bikes. My Triumph needed no major repairs. They fitted new tyres, a new chain, did a repair to the

Scottoiler tube, fitted a new engine temperature sensor, rebalanced the wheels and replaced an inlet valve shim, which was worn down by just one thousandth of an inch. So the bike survived from Istanbul to Australia, through the heartbreak of India, with the lightest of services.

The next morning I set off up the Brand Highway to start a 5900 mile journey around Australia that was scheduled to take no more than six days. A few hours later I left the vineyards of South Western Australia behind. The roadside became a thin slice of harsh vegetation, slicing through outback sheep stations where single families managed half a million acres or more and lived in breathtaking isolation. Beyond the Min-a-Ritchi Aboriginal bushes, Geraldton wax flowers and Banksia, the tribe at the end of the dirt would have been no more than six or seven people, plus a few migrant sheep shearers and black feller farm managers, living on an area larger than the square mileage of London.

Geraldton came into view, and I was greeted at the town limits by the sight of the big buxom women of the Geraldton Bowling Team. They were dressed in whites and straw boaters, studiously bowling. I watched for a moment to make the most of what was otherwise an awfully dull day. There are days when little happens that is worth remembering.

I rode all the rest of the day, and all day spoke just two words four times – "Thank you" to each of four gas station attendants. Even the words that still raged in my head without meaning or end had quietened. My body was calmed like a sail in a still wind and my heartbeat had slowed. It was good to be back on the road.

Geraldton is known in the area because of a ship that was wrecked on the coast there in 1706. Late one afternoon, 130 miles from Perth, there was a watery catastrophe of my own starting to happen. Only a week earlier, flooding in the north had closed the main highway and according to reports on the radio the waters had not yet subsided. The road undulated more and as the sun began to set the dirt on either side of the aphalt turned from the colour of sandalwood to the colour of rosewood. On my left, sections of countryside stretched to the sea; on my right, the desert started. It looked as if it spread forever.

The rains had fallen generously. In the past two years more rain had fallen than in the past two centuries. As I rode along my chosen track it was hard to imagine what it must have been like for the explorer Mr Simpson as he mapped this land over 100 years ago, never knowing if any water lay ahead that day or that week. I think, having motorbiked this section before on my Enfield, that there is a stretch of 180 miles coming up with nowhere to obtain fuel or water. In the unextraordinary nature of modern adventure, this is the closest I can get to a hardship worth comparing.

Diary: *Billabong Roadhouse*
It is getting dark, the bike is performing well and at the Billabong Roadhouse people say there is rain ahead. There is a cyclone off the coast nearby at Denham and it is producing strong winds. I phone ahead to the Overlander Roadhouse and book a room for the night. Just an hour left to ride. The roadhouse manager at Billabong tells me that

because of the recent rains, kangaroos have less reason to stray from their usual watering holes in search of others and so should not need to cross the road. But sheep still dart in the darkness before my lights, animals big enough to make me fall. This changes the focus of my anxieties. Now there is no longer any traffic, nor people, nor holes in the road, nor heat and blistering wind, but there is still the fallout of animals from Australia's hedgerows. There is little time, either, to spot small creatures that will have me sliding on their carcasses and innards if they are crushed by my wheels.

As I sat in my small Portacabin room at the Overlander Roadhouse before having a shower and dinner, a woman, perhaps in her late thirties or forties, passed by and greeted me. She had my mother's eyebrows. I responded and we started a conversation. We talked about this and that, until sitting beside me on my bed, she leaned over and held my hand and closed her eyes.

"I can see, you know," she said. "I can see the spirit within that also lies without and around and I can see yours. Do you want to know?" I nodded. "He is perfect and strong around you and very white. He is smiling and happy with his journey. He is happy because you are taking him, or he you, on a very exciting adventure in your life. He is laughing now." She paused, her eyes still closed.

"I see on your right a mountain lion, or is it a cougar? It is the cat that has the strength that dispels the mundane and the ineffectual. She is also the pacer and rides with you at speed." Again she paused, until after a few minutes of holding my arm she continued. "I see also on your left you have the bear. It is not the grizzly, nor the fun bear, it is the Alaskan brown bear that represents your strength, that IS your strength. The bear swipes at everything you feel you have no need of, and clears the way for the important things." Her eyes were still closed. She smiled in the way mystics smile and in the way the heads of mystics move, she rocked slightly.

"And above I see the eagle. High above, the eagle gives you your eyes, and it is from there that you will see - look ahead from there. The cougar is the leader and the bear your strength, and from the eagle comes the mastery of high vision. And one more thing - if ever you get a shiver in your spine as I am doing now, remember to believe what your spirits are telling you. It is not over yet for you, but listen and be aware and then your spirit will laugh and smile and sit behind you on your motorbike to protect you, and he will continue to enjoy the ride."

17

The farther north I rode, the hotter it became. I rode by Geraldton, Port Hedland, Broome and on towards Darwin. Each night I camped in the desert, where the day dawns not little by little but suddenly, and it is as hot as noon in an hour. There were no matins of birds in the morning, just rock partridge cocks chuckling over the waterless desolation.

There was only the giddy heat on the crown of the head. Flickering shrillness in tingling ears. A subtle glassiness of the sun. Hot sand-blinking eyes. Days upon end drowned in unceasing summer wilderness. More days spent with my thoughts suppurating in the silence and the sun, my life-force gently crisping.

I have been to places where trees are so tall that they touch the clouds, so still that all the water from the rains sluices through their leaves and drips on land below that has never been touched by the sun; where the eternal shadows below become so deep that creatures grow big eyes to see. But here the deserts were so vast that they disengaged all notions of reality. Sometimes there was not one single object, tree or rock, on which the eye could focus. Landscapes such as these turn straight lines into circles.

Diary: Somewhere in Australia

The next day the cyclone that lies off Denham, a short distance away, is growing bigger. There is water on the road north of here. This time last year a wall of water 20 feet high came down on Carnarvon. Truck drivers coming down from the north say I should be able to get through but that depends on whether it continues to rain, and it is still raining. It is now six o'clock and past dawn. I intend to ride at least 850 miles today.

70

Further on in Australia: Karratha to Willare Bridge Roadhouse

The mileage figures have improved a little but I'm still 300 miles down on what I had scheduled. I'm now 1100 miles down on my initial estimate for Australia, which it seems was a bit optimistic. Unless I ride late into the night there is no way of achieving today's target. The risk of hitting animals on the road is very high at night. Even though I have ridden here at night before on my Enfield journey, and now on this one, I know I'm pushing my luck.

At the Willare Bridge Roadhouse by the Fitzroy River, a little south of Derby, the locals tell me of cattle straying across the road further up. A lot of the cattle here are black. The nightmarish vision in my head is of me riding into the side of a ton of cow while trying to squeeze another 120 miles out of the schedule. And what then? Wrapped up bike, dead cow, injured rider with head jammed up cow's arse. At night I dream, but only for a short while in case the dreams are fearful. Sometimes my dreams ring of portent. At other times they are riddled with the clatter of idle thoughts. I twist and turn in my dreams, glad to be still alive. 130 miles short of Fitzroy Crossing, I stop at the roadhouse. I will try to reach Katherine by the following evening, 830 miles away. I think this is possible.

With restrictions on travelling at night, the logistics of getting around Australia are going to be difficult. Anything less than 700 miles a day will put me under pressure to ride very hard in the States, where at least I can ride day and night more easily. Right now I am questioning my planning ability. I have seriously underestimated the problems with animals on the roads. If I'd come here a little earlier I would have gained more daylight time, this being Australia's summer, but that would have coincided with the wet season in the north and the roads would have been impassable at the bridge points. The waters have only just receded now the dry season has started. Europe would have been colder and wetter, as would the States. Coping with the climatic needs of this project has been a juggling act in which the shape of the balls constantly changes in mid-air. I'll have to modify the schedule to 800 miles per day around Australia, with a 24 hour, non-stop ride down to Sydney, where there will be no animal problem. A couple of non-stop runs in the States will put me back on schedule and a non-stop run from Lisbon to London should clinch the record.

I am tired and I am nervous about napping. When I nap I don't want to wake up. I try to follow a fast car on the final ninety miles from the Broom turn off and sit happily behind him, but I then feel my eyes closing and I have an overwhelming need to sleep. My eyes shut and only a fierce shake of my head forces them back open. I stop and immediately I am asleep on the tank. Instinctively I wake myself, knowing that it is getting darker - the sun has set and I have fifteen minutes of light left. I know I should continue immediately but I hesitate for five minutes, wanting to sleep more. My discipline is slipping. Am I hanging on to this record by my finger tips? Is it slipping away from me?

I saw somewhere a baby iguana running across the road. It was carrying a Coke can, as if to its nest. Maybe this was a clever iguana and it realised that the can would make a container for water to last through a drought, I thought as I raced past. The aluminium can glinted in the sun. Even though I was under pressure to keep going and cover more miles, I couldn't resist turning back to investigate.

The iguana, now darting backwards and forwards across the road, wasn't carrying the can by choice. It had got its head stuck in the ring pull hole. It couldn't see where it was going and it couldn't eat or drink; in fact it would probably die soon. It was also quite funny - a Coke head with a difference.

I caught the little thing, and as it struggled I calmed it by stroking its back, and tried to ease the can off its head. It was stuck tight and I thought I might pull the creature's head off, but by moving the can carefully from side to side by the distance between its scales, I eased its neck out. I think it knew I was helping because now there was no struggling, just a pumping of its heart as if it was going to burst its body. Then its head popped out of the hole and the iguana shook itself and darted off into the undergrowth.

Diary: *Willare Bridge Roadhouse to Timber Creek*

I rode 700 miles today. In the Northern Territories there is no speed limit, which helped in the final stages before dark, and I concentrated on riding and dispensed with filming. I have to reach Sydney within three days from now to have a chance of achieving the record. I rode like the wind, from Willare Bridge to Fitzroy Crossing, then Halls Creek and from there to Kunnunara. I stopped only for breakfast at Fitzroy Crossing, coffee at Halls Creek and fuel at the other places. I spoke to no-one. Sometimes I think this causes too much introspection. I have to try not to be negative and to remain cheerful in my helmet for fourteen hours a day. I am in solitary confinement on this journey. Up at dawn, ride all day, finish into the night, eat and sleep.

Australia is a world where ancient hills seem to take on the contours of giant marsupials, carved out of time; their age-old evolution frozen in geomorphic form. According to Aboriginal lore, rivers are the tracks of the rainbow serpent and the Milky Way is the river of the sky where, after the rainbow serpent has swallowed the sun, people go and fish for stingrays and turtles. The stars are their campfires.

At Fitzroy Crossing I had telephone calls to make. Outside the phone box, Aborigines kicked each other's heads as if trying to score a goal. The last time I used this very same phone I was riding my Enfield around the world and the scene was the same then. Same acts, different people drop-kicking each other at my feet. Same type of thick skull cushioning the fall of a heavy rock dropped by an irate wife on to her husband's head. Games of life and love. Same memories' but more distant.

I stayed that time with friends near Sydney and woke up with my hostess standing over me, wanting me. She had blue eyes, a nice round face and lips that could have sealed an envelope at arms length. I stripped off her nightdress and sank hard between her big white thighs; six months of celibacy ended then. We loved each other briefly, and talked and slept and dreamed in each other's arms.

My adventures seem to shift from stultifying numbness at one extreme to rare moments of triumphantly achieved meaning at the other. I feel then that happiness is contingent on our believing that life has meaning, even if this is not true. I think all of my journeys have been about either searching for a beautiful woman, or impressing my worth on the one I have. A man I once met in the port of Latvia in Syria told me a story.

"It ees all about a warrior who goes to ze war to protect ees land and ees country, and it ees his woman, no, ees princess who waits for ees return. But the enemy falsely sends news of his slaying and ze princess throws herself from ze battlements to her death. When he returns, he ees so stricken with ze grief that he knows he must continue to be wandering theese lands until he finds another princess. It ees good story eh? It ees what each of us here feel about theese side of our lives."

18

Now I was on the final stretch of the Australian section. Here the road narrowed to Timber Creek. After dark I found myself among herds of cattle that were trampling across the road to escape small fires in the bush. I nearly skinned the hide off one steer. I had to brake violently and pulled up about two feet from his side. He didn't flinch, but my heart nearly stopped beating. Smoke made blacker by the night stung my nostrils and blew across the way. I knew how stupid it was to ride fast at night so after that I rode cautiously, winding around potholes in a road that was surfaced with hard-baked clay.

Later that night a small bird flew up and crashed into my boot. I rode back to find him breathing hard by the side of the road. I picked him up, but his neck was broken. In the dark silence, punctuated by crickets and the lights from my bike, I felt very sad. The bush fires in the distance were spreading closer to the roadside. There was confusion in the bush and many birds lined the road, some darting in front of me. The bird I had injured had a face like an owl. I flattened out some grass and made him comfortable to die.

I rode on more carefully. The roadhouse at Timber Creek was not far away. Four hours later I turned into the Wayside Motel Roadhouse, flipped down my kickstand and slumped down on to the tank. I was exhausted and didn't think I could eat, but I knew that if I starved myself I would become weak and confused.

In the roadhouse, the men at the bar wanted to know everything about me. One man had a mouth so big he could have gripped a bunch of bananas between his lips, and his nose was so long he could have directed the traffic without using his arms. I was in no mood for stupid questions. I had just ridden 700 miles and if I was going to reach Sydney in four days I would have to ride an even greater distance than that each day.

Mister Banana Mouth came over to talk to me, as I knew he would. Sometimes, to escape from the unbearable heaviness of such dinner-table conversation, I leave my head talking on my body to answer questions of where and why and the certifiable nature of such a quest, and revisit with my thoughts the dusty roads I have been riding on.

"So what's it like mate, the route to yer likin', I drive a truck meself, wouldn't catch me on a bike to save me life, *ooh nooo,* dangerous things wot with the roos an all, my wife an all, kids an all...you'd be better off in a car, expensive hobby must 'av cost a bob or two...better off with a proper job...so what do you do for a living?...not-that-tits any of my business, just being friendly an all..."

The slowness of such a dull conversation, hunched so close to me, kept my head talking in a severed sort of way. But I was really tracing along fields of wheat and paddies of glistening water, sometimes flying overhead watching myself riding fast on my bike. It's a slow-motion silent movie with flashes of colour, a blue sea-green of gathering birds. I can see myself mouthing shapes of yes and no, a shrug of my shoulders, a smile, a face contorting to suit the conversation. It is all of no consequence, this compliance.

"I'm a bit tired and I'd like five minutes to myself to get over the day," I said.

"Know exactly what you mean Pom, feel jus' the same after a day in the truck, need to wind down, s'funny but people don't understand, I remember when...funny you should say that...another beer...hey fellers the Pom's going round the world...round the bend if you ask me...*ha, ha...what a nutter... takes the biscuit... might be catching...ha ha... "*

19

Diary: Timber Creek to Katherine
I left Timber Creek after six because the sun rises later in the north. I had slept well. A car overtook me and I rode close behind it to have some protection from the kangaroos. I rode at 100 mph and more. I reckoned I might make up a little time, although there is always something that slows me down - stopping to write a diary note takes up 30 minutes, and that is 50 miles lost. It's not enough, never enough. However hard I try, I do not match the expectations of my schedule, which I now realise is unrealistic. Nothing is as certain as I once thought it was.

From time to time I rode fast. The road surface was uneven and there were only two lanes, but there was no other traffic. I had the road all to myself. I knew that there were animals near the roadside, but I couldn't see them. I had hardly seen them at night, and not at all during the day, so the chance of a collision was low. The run was exhilarating and fast enough. There is only so much heart to be had in one day, so I restrained my bravura and settled for a cruise.

I rode hard all day, again talking to no-one, hardly stopping to see, hearing only the throaty purring of the engine and the exhaust, the wind rushing through my helmet, the sound of the tyres against different road surfaces, swishing and bracing, hammering, and sometimes scattering the dust.

After eighteen hours on the bike, looking straight ahead was like squinting into the sun. The horizon dissolved into whiteness and the road was a strip of asphalt, with lines of sand fringing the grey. I was alone on the road on endless plains, like a bug on the windscreen of life. I slowed as I passed Alice Springs, which was sheltered by a rim of bluffs and beautifully placed in the centre of such a grand land mass. There was no time to stop. I had to keep going.

"You are a pathetic kind of traveller, travelling and not seeing. You see no places of interest. You take me everywhere and yet you go nowhere. I do not stand in the sea up to my knees. Always I am on your back."

"In the sea the fish announce the music. At night the moon begins to sleep."

"Stop Zenning me for Chrissake, just slow down and have a look around."

"If I slow down I don't get the record and my journey will be no different to any of the others."

"So what? No-one will think it's important. Why do you crave this attention? You don't have anything original to say..."

"That depends on you."

"Why?"

"Whether you want to be impressed by me, or anyone for that matter."

"Go on then, give it a try. Impress me."

"The apple falls. The tortoise marches to the circus."

"What does that mean?"

"It doesn't have to mean anything."

"Oh, that's really impressive. What else have you got up your sleeve?"

"The interplay of opposites. If you want to achieve something you have to start with the opposite. For example, those who claim to be brave must also profess to be weak. Those who say they are strong, must also say they are meek"

"Get outta here..."

"It's to do with the unity of all things. I've heard it said that everything is to do with opposites. Fast and slow, for example. You cannot be fast without first being slow."

Diary: Threeways Roadhouse

Left at eight. I have only eleven hours of daylight in which to ride safely, nine and a half hours after fuel stops, and even less after an occasional coffee break. It will be a good average to ride 670 miles in nine hours.

Nine hours later I switched off the engine. I had talked to no-one, heard only the pistons thrashing, felt only the rumble of hard rubber on road.

20

"You are condemned to freedom my friend," said my invisible companion.

My senses were blazing. The rhythm of the day's ride had set up a kind of oscillation in my head. Never in the history of a journey so short had anyone ruminated so much about nothing. No, not quite true. Nothing should read *'nothingness'.* Anyway, there are writers who write about journeys around a friend's back garden. They write about minutiae, at length about the folds of their trousers. I am also absorbed by the minuteness of my project perhaps. It would have been easier to describe this journey in an edible form; a sausage for a paragraph, a slice of bacon for a chapter heading. Chew impregnated corners of a page and be transported to another world.

"It is the clockmaker's pendulum. The earth is a bob, where each oscillation of history is repeated again and again and bounced off the moon."

"Off the moon?!"

"The earth is tossed by the sun. It is the circus act of this collosal mechanism. It is the epoch of the ages and it happens every day."

"Tell me then if you're so clever, and forgive me if I appear cliched, but am I a man dreaming he is a butterfly or a butterfly dreaming he is a man?"

"The answer is beyond human knowing."

"Your words are studded with hints and riddles. How do you interpret *'I wander through each dirty street, Near where the dirty Thames does flow, And on each human face I meet, Marks of weakness, marks of woe...'* Life seems to be full of people obsessed with the idea that misery will never end. Is cosmology really the study of the universe or of a machine which greases our bristles and fills our snouts?"

"The curse of our civilisation is boredom. Put most people in the middle of a desert and they would go mad. They don't have much of an idea of who they are. They are prisoners in their own minds."

"I see only strained faces, roughly ridden faces, distracted from distraction by distraction. Like them, I don't have any visionary faculty because like most men, I live too intensely, under too much pressure to get and spend. Men and bits of paper blowing about in a cold wind. I have to shout, to be heard above the crowd, *what do I do to be saved?*"

"If you're talking about salvation, forget it. Heaven after death is spurious. The real way is more life, more consciousness. Life is an ordeal that has to be endured. Suicide or mind suicide, or the seeking of some other fantastical domicile, is not the answer. Go deeper into real life where the way home is not necessarily the way back."

"I don't always understand you, meaning I can't always sift through your nonsense. Your reasoning is powerful, but my love is stronger."

"That's a non sequitur if ever there was one."

"Now it's your turn not to understand. Linear time is a false perception. It is we who make up the minutes and the days. My love is stronger than my reason. When my Dad was dying, he was rambling in his head but not his heart, almost disconnecting himself from the physical world before my eyes. When I said to him, *'Dad I love you so much'*, he responded by some celestial reflex and said, *'Son, I love you more'*. Answers like that are relayed faster than the speed of thought. Of course his love was stronger, he made me."

"This is completely out of context. He's not dead."

"I know, but he soon will be, and that's what he will say." And he did.

21

Somewhere in the desert I stopped the bike. The wind swooped around me with whispers and caresses. The road smelled of dust and hot stones, all bathed in an ancient brooding light, the kind of light you set sail in. The sun began to set and the wind calmed. I climbed up on to the bike and stood on the seat. Higher by three feet, I was suddenly in another world. Wherever I looked I could see flat plains. I imagined I could see the curvature of the earth. I looked over the acacia bushes nearest to the road, and astonishingly, another hundred million came into view, little bushes that spotted the red clay soil in every direction for as far as could be seen.

There was no sound from the engine now and I became aware of how quiet this journey could be. Serenity comes in small moments of contemplation. Everyone needs to go where they will not be disturbed, yet by simply being, they were already there. It is the great irony of rides like this that the engine both takes you to and separates you from that quiet place of reason.

In a few breaths I felt perfect detachment from the world. Ignorance had given me the fearlessness to get here, but seeing such vast emptiness made me afraid. Stilled by the silence, relieved of movement, I tried for a moment of vision. Great sages would probably have said that if they had been given a fast bike to blow a breeze around their parchment and quills, they too would have ridden a million miles for a few seconds of heaven.

It is now night and I ride past cattle wandering across the track, but so far no kangaroos. I had intended to ride through the night, but the locals shook their heads and stared into their beer.

"Wild horses," said one. "They shoot out from the dark don't they? They say if you see the animal you're all right, but it's the ones you don't see that'll get you."

"Straight impact," said another, thwacking his hands together. So it is the usual Aussie steak, chips and salad seasoned with e-mails, and straight to bed.

Today I met someone I had spoken to six years ago on the road leading up to Ayers Rock. I allowed myself ten minutes to chat, but promised to see him again in a couple of years time. Spray-painted on bridges over busy rush-hour intersections are the words *'Good Morning Lemmings'*.

22

In the Northern Territories I understood that there was no speed limit, so from time to time I rode at a ton-forty. I was to learn later that I had been misinformed. Nonetheless the ride was exhilarating and well controlled. You would think that to ride at such speed would require one to be a little out of control, but to fall at such speed would probably mean death. So the control is absolute.

The road surface was not even and there were just two lanes. There was no other traffic. I suspected that there were animals a little way off the roadside, but I couldn't see them. I had hardly seen any at night, and none at all during the day, so I thought the chance of a collision was small. It was wonderful to ride so fast, and also terrible. To pursue such speed, knowing that a wobble could mean the end of life, was intoxicating. Life is intoxicating, but so is the prospect of death. To stay alive on a motorbike, everything has to be calm. To die riding is the warrior way to go, but a little foolish.

It felt easier to reach high speeds this time. The route to 130 miles per hour was unremarkable. The power of the engine, the throaty torque surging like an immense lung-filling breath, carried me there smoothly. It took a while to edge from 138 mph to 141 mph, and then to creep on by degrees up the clock. The rear sprocket had been replaced with one that was a tooth smaller and the lower gearing restricted my top speed slightly, but slowly, after several miles, and on the third attempt, on a straight and empty road in northern Australia, I wound the bike up to its absolute maximum speed of 154mph and approached one-fifth the speed of sound.

As had now become the pattern, I rode hard all day, talking to no one, not stopping to see, hearing only the purring of the machine, the wind rushing through my helmet, the sound of tyres against the road. In the morning I had left the Threeways Roadhouse at the junction of the Barkly and Stuart Highways. At nightfall I would sleep at the Cadney Park Roadhouse south of Alice, close to the Adelaide to Alice Springs railway line and a couple of hours ride north of Coober Pedy.

My kind hosts at Cadney Park allowed me to e-mail by linking through their fax machine with my PC. I ate a steak the size of a fat man's face. I slept soundly, for I knew the next stretch of the journey was going to be hard. I didn't know it then, but I was about to ride from Cadney Park to Sydney more or less non-stop, a distance of 1786 miles, in 39 hours.

A hundred miles on I rode into Coober Pedy, Australia's foremost opal mining town. Its outskirts were littered with pyramid-shaped piles of cream-coloured earth. They dotted the landscape, stretching to the horizon, pockets of territory penned and labelled, the dreams of miners.

In a town like Coober Pedy, weird finds weird normal. I stopped to video a strange hopper and conveyor belt contraption on a trailer and the driver came over and started chatting. It was a noodle machine, about twenty metres long, and it sifted excavated dirt and passed it through an ultraviolet darkroom onboard to find opals that had been missed the first time. John, the driver and owner of his enterprise, said it cost a hundred grand a year in diesel alone to run the show, and he would net maybe three times that amount in opals in an average year. He lived in a cave down the road and offered to put me up for the night. But I couldn't stop.

As we chatted in the heat, an older guy, stockier, drove up and was introduced to me as Peter. He was a kangaroo shooter who culled roos for a living. He said it was for the benefit of the sheep farmers.

"The roos eat all the grass see, and the cattle an' sheep perish," he said. "On a good night I can kill maybe a ton an' half. Fifty-one roos." He could see I was interested and he started to fold a roll-up. I was desperate for conversation with anyone other than my invisible friend.

"Yeah, see," he said, lighting up his cigarette, "we load 'em on the back of the truck and drive 'em back to town where they're eaten as a local delicacy." He smiled when he saw my face.

I was quiet and he seemed to join me for a moment. There was a sense of two people who had spent much time alone and were happy with life's silences. He turned to me with a 'yup' to voice-activate us back to conversation.

"That's the way....an' roos can smell water from miles away ya know an' dig deep into stream beds to the artesian water supply. They're survivors ya know, and as such they're a difficult pest to eradicate." He paused. "If we didn't cull tha fackers, Aus-traa-liaa," he drawled, "would be overrun."

Around me little piles of dirt the colour of semen stood like goose pimples, commemorating the sweat of men underground. It was almost a mating display; the bigger the pile, the bigger the probability that you got the opal. Get your money, get your woman.

"I'll tell yer something else yer don't know mate." He shifted from one foot to the other and spat out his roll-up. "Ya know, wild cats find a rabbit warren durin' the breedin' season, an' they dig their own hole in the centre an' allow the baby rabbits to come up to the surface, well they have a look around an' see the cat. Knowing no better, they think he's quite normal and accept his presence. But that's not it, matey. Later, when the cat wants a snack, he waits for a rabbit to nosey up to 'im, yer know, to say good on yer for looking after us Mister Cat and bosh, that fackin' cat he goes an' he swipes a baby. Down the hatch mate an' no one's the wiser. The cat he don't have to hunt, he just has to be accepted - an' it's an example of duplicity at its best or worse, depending on yer perspective." He nodded to the dirt. "Like them poor bastards down there. It's fifty degrees ya know but yer get yer big dirt an' yer 'ome an' dry. That's why she's 'ere." He looked over at a tight-bottomed young woman. "Yeah, that Sheila'll go down on ya if ya stick around overnight, fine girl, we need more like her round these parts."

I nearly stayed. But I had to go. I had already spent two hours filming and chatting. By lunchtime I had ridden just 100 miles.

23

I rode past the Woomera rocket launch site near Pimba and by five had passed through the mining town of Port Augusta, 350 miles down the road from Coober Pedy. I stopped only to refuel. There was not much light left; it was winter in Australia, and daylight hours were lessening. And because I was travelling east, I was losing time relative to GMT. Farther east I would be docked another thirty minutes as I crossed from South Australia into New South Wales.

There was little chance of meeting wildlife on the road now because it had been raining and the animals would be content to graze. They only came to the road when the land was parched, because they knew moisture could be licked off the road surface. The road also acted as a conduit and ran the morning dew off to the roadside, so all the juicy bushes grew there.

By late evening I had ridden another 250 miles and reached Adelaide. I stopped there for coffee before setting off up the hill out of town to find the highway to Melbourne, which was more than 500 miles away. The weather was cold and rain was falling hard. I was beginning to wobble again and my eyes were beginning to close. I saw a roadside truck stop coming up.

"Hey look, paaal! Wake up wake up, wakey wakey you're fallin' asleep boy." The reflection in my helmet had squeezed itself out of my head.

"Com'n see the neon sign flashing in the rain."

"I don't see it" I said, rubbing my eyes.

"Course you do, it reads 'Welcome to the Room of Dryness and Warmth."

"It does?" I was so tired that I could have been hallucinating. A man leapt out and flagged me down.

"There's a plate of chips and there's sex for you inside."

"There is?"

"Course there is mate, you're getting there ain't you, across the divide."

"You are so pretentious."

"As in Rome matey...anyway, what do you reckon, sex AND chips!!"

I had to stop. If I closed my eyes again I would not wake. If I stayed on the bike I had to listen to madness. How would it feel to die in my sleep? Would there be any pain?

"No pain mate, just a room of warm girls and chips. Chips, chips, frites, french fries and everywhere with bowls of mayo for finger lickin' dippin."

"Yeah, but sex like that is just a hollow experience."

"True right enough, but lighten up. As a hollow experience it's one of the best."

I parked the bike and followed the man into the roadhouse.

"You sit down there son," the old man said. *"Eat your chips and tell your mother about it later."*

Funny, that's what my Dad used to say to me when I wanted to tell him about my life. I was suddenly alone amidst the spirits of quietness. It was the dead of night. I lay down behind the table and slept.

I slept from midnight until three o'clock in the morning. I rose very sleepily, jumped back on the bike and rode in rain and night towards Melbourne. I rode all night until dawn, across the rolling cattle pastures of lowland Victoria. Heavy morning mists covered the road, but I kept on going. I dashed into the city at midday, just in time for a press call at the Triumph dealership, and grabbed another couple of TV shows and a coffee.

Within the hour I had set off again for Sydney. I had been riding for a day, a night, and half a day. I had 550 miles still to go, and I had to arrive in Sydney before eleven that evening to check my bike in at customs for an early morning flight to Christchurch, New Zealand. I rode fast and hard, and twice fell asleep again on the move at a speed of 75 mph. The first time I jerked awake and sat upright, but the second time I stayed asleep a fraction longer than my survival instinct said was sane. So I pulled into a layby and slept for an hour on the tank. Or was it ten minutes?

I woke in time to see the sun setting. I rode harder and faster into the night and more rain. Across Victoria and into South Australia, riding hard, really hard, passing hedgerows and trees and five-barred gates in a blur; creosoted telegraph poles rhythmically marking my passage past the cattle and the dog-walkers and driveways that joined the road to the horizon. It was beginning to hurt, so much aching.

Then I saw the lights of Sydney in the distance and followed signs for the airport. I made it to the freighters just in time, checked in, weighed the machine and signed the paperwork. Thirty minutes later and I would have missed the flight. Two hours and twenty minutes later I was in New Zealand.

In Christchurch it was raining and I had to climb back on the bike and start another day's ride. Please, when will it stop? Please, I want it to stop. Please spirit, let me stop.

I have nearly another 240 miles to ride to the ferry at Picton on the north end of South Island, and I wonder if this madness will ever end. I have no mind left to spare; no mind to think. Just enough to breathe and balance, to grip my clutch lever and wring the neck of my throttle. No more story. Too tired. Ending; nearly ending.

24

I just made the eight-thirty flight from Sydney to Christchurch and arrived at one-thirty in the afternoon. Customs knew in advance of my arrival, and the bike was to be cleared by three o'clock. Both national TV news channels were waiting to do interviews, and although I didn't know it then, every paper, TV channel and major radio station had put someone on the story.

It was raining when I left the airport, and by five in the afternoon the sky was very overcast. I suspected that it would be foggy down the road. The distance to the Wellington ferry at Picton was 217 miles, and I had to be there before the ferry left at nine-thirty that evening.

For the first thirty miles the route was flat without sharp bends. Even in the rain the scenery by the road was gentle; green pastures and rolling fields of sheep and cattle, helpfully fenced in so that round-the-world bikers could pass unimpeded. But soon it was dark. It was midwinter in the southern hemisphere, less than a month away from the shortest day of the year. On the other side of the world the days would be moving into summer. By Cheviot it was raining very hard. I stopped in a tea room, a common sight in New Zealand, like the Casa de Te houses in Welsh Patagonia. I ordered a coffee and watched myself on the six o'clock news. "Hello Dad!" I said quietly.

I had three hours still to ride to get to the ferry when a fierce storm blew up. Wind blew and rain peppered my helmet. I had to keep wiping my visor clear of water to see where I was going. The plastic was badly scratched and I was finding it difficult to make out the road, but if I had my visor up the rain stung my eyes. The road twisted and turned. I wound the bike round tightening corners, up and down the foothills, across the Hurunui River and then the Waiau River and on with the time ticking away. If I missed this ferry I would lose a day.

I rode hard, still reeling from the last thirty-nine hours and 1800 miles across New South Wales. I began to panic, thinking that I might miss the ferry, so I rode even harder and faster. At Kaikoura the road leaned close by a sea that was bashing against the rocks in the light of a moon half obscured by clouds. As the roads straightened out, with only occasional bends, my average speed rose and I began to think I might make it in time.

I rushed on past Seddon and Blenheim, and then, twenty miles before Picton, the black skies suddenly unleashed a storm of such intensity that I had to stop. Thirty minutes to go and the record could be lost. My flight was booked from Auckland to Anchorage and I was trapped here in this ferocious storm. I stopped and held on to the bike. The rain was beating and the wind blew the tops of trees down on to the road. It was a storm to lift the rafters.

I got back on the bike and tried again, in a sea of rain. Somehow I stayed upright and set off. I was not going to miss this ferry: I dare not. I was down to the last couple of minutes when I reached Picton.

"It's about to leave," said the man at the ticket counter. "If you run to the terminal building, and you're lucky, you might still get on."

I rode fast to the entrance and ran to the counter. "Can I get on the ferry?" I asked, breathless. "Am I too late?" It was fifteen minutes past nine.

"We've closed the hold," said the girl at the desk. "I'm sorry, it'll have to be tomorrow."

"But, I'm riding around the world..."

"I'm sorry, but there's nothing I can do," the girl said.
My God. After all that. I was on the brink of tears. If crying could have got me on board, I would easily have obliged.

"Maybe I can speak to the Captain?"

"You can't, but I can," said a voice from behind me. "I'm the first mate. I saw you on TV tonight. I'm just boarding

94

myself. Stay here and we'll give you a call. I'll see if the old man will bend the rules." I was speechless. So grateful. I sat down and waited. Closed my eyes. Shallow breathing. Felt faint. Silly really. More minutes passed. The phone at the front desk rang and the girl answered it.

"You cut it fine, didn't you? They're opening the bow for you," she said smiling, and handed me a sheet of paper. "Would you sign this for my brother?"

25

I was ravenous, and made for the cafeteria. I ate a meal of chicken and chips and washed it down with a cup of sweet tea. The faster I ate the sooner I would shit, and the more time I would have to sleep. As the harbour lights edged out of sight and the channel broadened into the strait, I made two phone calls. There were only two people in my life now, the mother of my unborn child and my Dad. One was full of anxious cooings, her tongue speaking love; the other was full of tight-lipped cheer; and both wanted to have me home soon. She, back home, made my life stand still, only to rush after me like a sweet breeze when we were apart. He, at 84, had shown me what it was to be devoid of ego, a trait not followed through by his son.

"The Cook Strait," he said. "By jingo, and then off to Alaska the next day. Well by jove," and he clicked his teeth in the way he sometimes did. "You're the hardest man I know, son." This was a distinct improvement over what he had once thought. My Dad used to think I was a spaceman, and in a sense he was right. Dads are rarely wrong.

As the ferry crossed the Strait to the North Island of New Zealand, I slept for an hour and then rose at midnight to start another day. Ross Burrell, PR trouble-shooter for Mobil New Zealand, was to meet me at Wellington and schedule the media for the rest of my stay on the island. When I disembarked he drove to his house and I followed. He had a spacious high-level flat overlooking the city. After tea and toast with Ross I set off north. Wellington looked almost quaint, as cityscapes go, dressed in deep night. I glanced back again and it was gone.

Several times I stopped, to wake and screw my eyes into shape so that they could see. The rain was spitting steel rods of fine spray. A month's rain fell that night, and I was riding into a front that was moving south from Auckland to meet and make mischief with the roaring forties.

My bike was scheduled to leave Auckland for Anchorage later in the afternoon, and I was going to have to ride over 400 miles through the night to make up the day's quota, having ridden 217 miles since Christchurch. The 1700 miles I had covered over the previous 36 hours were still aching in my body. I began to feel floaty and detached. Not since Equador had I felt as exhausted as I felt now. That dreadful time on the Pan Americana had become the benchmark for hard riding. I felt I was beginning to drift away.

By the time I reached the town of Bulls, less than a hundred miles from Wellington, I was riding weakly and had needed more stops than usual. For half the night I had recorded a poor average speed. I was beginning to wobble. I resolved to sleep for a solid hour and damn my schedule. I stopped on a garage forecourt, switched off the engine, slumped forward, chest on the tank, and instantly fell into a deep sleep. It must have been odd for people fuelling their cars to see me there, arms hanging down like a dead man, head still in my helmet, boots on, ready to go.

I woke just before dawn feeling revitalised. I reckoned I had been out for one and a half hours. I started the bike and set off immediately, less than a minute after waking. The rain had stopped, and now I could see where I was going. There were foggy patches over the desert plateau around Lake Taupo, but otherwise the going was good. I continued through Turangi, with Nganruhoe mountain looming high on my left. I was feeling fit, strong, relaxed and no longer tired. My face was dirty and wind-streaked from leaky eyes. As I descended towards a vast stretch of water, I could see mist still hanging around volcanic pimples that pushed upwards into the air like noses sniffing their dribbles. I weaved and cornered around hills of black rock.

Through the fogs and past Lake Taupo I rode and rode, taking little time to look around. I was soon on the point of exhaustion again, but now I rode with a kind of hardness, wearied by the journey, embattled by the traffic, emboldened by the knowledge that even though I had only just passed the antipodal point in the journey, I was approaching the last major leg before home. On I went through Tokoroa and Putaruru before finally descending into green farming country around Hamilton, where the sheep for which this pasture land is famous stood stuffing themselves. In the distance they had looked like fat maggots. I rode on and on - Morrinsville, Huntly, Manukau, into the city limits of Auckland, and fast to the airport. There, with the help of Triumph contacts and friends of friends, I put the bike into the hands of the freighters. The bike was to go via Seattle to Anchorage in Alaska, and I was to fly there in the early hours of the following morning. There was time to rest, and count the days to when this journey would end.

Diary: Auckland

I am in a warm house in Auckland, bathed and rested. After catching up with my stories I will sleep. In my room, alone, I sit down and feel my body reacting to what it has gone through. I can feel myself vibrating inside. Resonating. Before I sleep my eyes oscillate in their sockets like a nervous tic. One minute I am riding hard at speed, facing possible death, and the next minute I am motionless and safe, tucked up in bed. No time to slow down, just go fast or stop. Sometimes I wake from sleep and I am still shaking. I look out over the rooftops of houses on the outskirts of Auckland. I don't know if I am dreaming or not.

26

"Okay, c'mon then, spit it out, tell us all exactly why you do it. Fill us in with the secret formula, you know, the hero goo...God it's so sick-making when all they ever say, these

warrior ginks, is because it's there. Because WHAT for Chrissake is THERE? I mean, pleeease, ill-um-inate-me...we know it's there, it's on the TV, it's on the Internet, people go on guided tours to the top of Everest, people do everything so we know it's there. Tell me something about motor-biking around the world that I don't know."

There was scoffing in the air. Little bubbles of dissent sank around me like darkness, making it hard for me to think.

"You're right. We do know it's *there...*"

"Okay then, so it's because you want to prove the big man in you and say to the world, hey look at me guys, I can do this and you can't. Is that it Mister Big Shot?"

"No it's not that at all. It's because the cherry blossom is falling."

"Oh right. Absolutely right on. And there's a tree walking across the road. Of course, why didn't I think of that? You're dreaming. No, you're on drugs mate. Your rationality has done a long-distance runner. You and your one-handed clap crap. I'm not buying it. I'm not even going to ask."

"But it's so simple. I'm just making assumptions, big generalisations."

"Oh yeah, that's just saying 'please like the way I think because I'm a nice guy' - I'm there before you man."

"You are the most cynical self."

"Truthful self."

"Well, thank goodness I have that. Without you I would have no innocence to parry with. To be all-wise is to be without foolishness, and you need a bit of that to be brave."

"Prevaricator."

"The easy way would have been to describe this journey as one of physical troughs and bumps - you know, where I ate, where I tinkered with the engine, reciting adventures from some 'Boy's Own' story. How I escaped with a bullet lodged in my head. But I'm through with that. I've come out the other side."

I was trying too hard to explain myself. My head was hurting with these inane conversations. Outside, the wind whipped up and the cherry blossom rained down in clusters. In my dream I was knee-deep in blossom, and I knew that if I stayed there long enough, I would be buried in it and would suffocate. This journey was all about time. Time to ride and time to rest. A time to fart, a time to eat. Every minute of my reality prescribed in linear form.

"Shit!" I jumped up in my bed, suddenly remembering, and looked at the darkness outside. "Bloody hell!" Was that the time? Why was it so dark? I'd only been asleep for a few moments. It seemed like hours. Was it time to go? I fumbled for my clock and then I saw my flight tickets and remembered. No bike to ride tonight. I could have the luxury of more sleep.

"Hang on. You've got me here now, out of your head, and you expect me to go away without an answer?"

"If the whole of the human body were reduced to nuclear density, it would be the size of a pin head."

I looked around at the plainly decorated walls, my pile of clothes in the corner, saddlebags and leathers. I realise the absurdity of this situation. Talking to myself on my bike, in my sleep, in my dreams. But, as the journey progresses, it is like a photograph of another world becoming visible in the developer. I see a face laughing at me laughing at him. At the unbearableness of the lightness of our being. Then I strain my eyes until I think I see atoms.

27

The motorcyclist asked the Zen master why he searched, and the master replied, *"Because the rain beats down on the leaves of willow trees and sometimes they bend and break."*

And the motorcyclist asked what this meant, and the master said nothing, as if to say that sometimes *nothing* is the answer, that there is no *answer* and if there is, it is *nothing*.

28

There is a form of meditation called Shikan-taza which is a state of concentrated awareness. It is a fitting way of thinking when facing death; it is neither hurried, nor uptight and tense; nor too relaxed. This is the state of mind I need to be in.

I am imagining myself back in India on the road crossing the Deccan Plateau. I'm riding along the highway on my bike.

I hear the faint sound of the engine purring through the layers of helmet and clothes, and feel the rumble of the road through the suspension and the seat. The wind is in my face, but it neither chills nor burns. Suddenly, I see people lying on the side of the road. Their feet are sticking out from under a blanket. Traffic is stopping in confusion. Other people are beginning to wander about between the vehicles to have a look. As I ride past, I see blood on the socks of the people lying under the blankets, and by the veins in their legs I know them to be old.

I am not blind nor deaf, but I am biking around the world quickly, and I see all this from the corner of my eye as I pass. My mind is not held long by these impressions. They are like a water-colour wash of images. It is as if they were always there, waiting for me to pass by.

The moon rises. It is a golden chair sitting on top of a bush. Then it is a sail, gilded by the unseen sun. When I look up at the stars they are still there. In my dream there is a wavering silver form. It is not speaking, and yet somehow I understand the words. Sometimes it is better to stay still and let the answers come to you. Why should you not hear the sound of colours or see music floating past your eyes?

Remember that you are a fusion of the stallion and the ocelot. It is only necessary to have someone believe in you to help you believe in yourself. If you fail or if the small triumphs you perform are not recognised, then you have to believe that there is still some person who thinks of you as a god and a monument; the finest fabric woven into a fairy tale of dreams. You do not need more. There is a moment when the bridge of air becomes stone, for that person to walk across and touch you.

29

Diary: On the flight to Alaska

The next day I am on the flight to America. People I speak to tell me to watch for elk and moose. They rush out like kangaroos and are blinded by headlights. I am hoping for a quick end to this project, but not like that. Instead, I intend to ride with the wind at my back for as long as I can make it blow.

30

Diary: Service at Don's Bike Shop in Anchorage, Alaska

At breakfast time a truck covered with motorbike logos arrives below my window. The Triumph guys take me to pick up the bike from the airport. The bike is released by the customs superintendent at United Airlines cargo at two in the afternoon. I ride it straight to the Triumph shop for Mike the mechanic to work on the tyres and accelerator cable. It takes him three hours to sort things out. I don't want to rush him as he's clearly doing a thorough job. A TV crew arrives. Mike sees a small problem: the oil sump drain plug needs replacing. Another TV crew turns up. The tyres are not on the wheels, but otherwise we are close to being on schedule. I feel fit and strong and after a night's sleep, well rested. The tyres have arrived and the Triumph team are all over the bike, checking everything.

Don, the boss of the Anchorage Motorcycle Shop, organised the service, having had a call from Triumph in the UK. The journey south is going to be arduous and the mechanics on the project must not fail me. I need to be away as soon as possible. I shall not sleep much tonight, as I need to make the most of the long daylight hours. My schedule requires me to ride over 1000 miles in each 24-hour period, from Alaska across British Columbia, north-west United States, the Midwest to Texas to my next service stop at San Antonio, and then north-east to New York. On the radio the weather forecast is good. The news tells of a twister directly on my route in Austin, Texas, which has flattened a village and killed thirty people. The clock is still ticking, but by half past five the service is completed and I am able to go. The late afternoon is sunny and warm, and the traffic in Anchorage is at what passes for its rush-hour peak. There are no queues, no gridlock. Hardly India. Not even a bit rushed.

Away from the city, I rode amid scenes of tremendous beauty. There were glorious mountain escarpments tipped with snow, hard-edged against an ice-cutting blue sky. My back wheel now faced the Arctic and my front wheel faced home. The panorama around most corners looked like a film in Cinemascope. All around me were mountain ridges covered with forests of pine and juniper up to the snowline.

Occasional scrub poked through the whiteness on outcrops of rock, and the horizon that now prevailed was like the serrated edge of desert ridges. I was witness to such splendour that sometimes I had to stop and sit beside my bike and stare at it, deadline or not.

31

"Okay then son, I'm going to ask the most obvious question of all." I looked around, surprised. There was no-one near. I was alone. Somehow the voice in my head had sounded more real than before, its resonance gaining a down-to-earth quality of such familiarity that I felt unnerved. It had sounded like someone very close to me. It had sounded like my Dad.

"Go on then," I heard him say. I relaxed. I could always talk to him; could always try out some theory or chew the philosophical cud. With him there was never any fear of intellectual retribution for saying something stupid. If the methodology didn't fit the meaning, he wouldn't contradict and we'd find a way to accommodate each other's views. He was a gentleman. You have to try and make sense of it all with your Dad.

There was no-one around to see me talking to myself, just some large black birds that chirrupped and trees that stood silently in the still air.

"So come on son, what's it all about? What's the point of riding around the world so fast that you don't see anything?"

I had always struggled with his pragmatism. I loved him but he annoyed me. He sat there with his stockinged feet and his jug of ale and his silly grin. When the ale came out I could say anything and he would think me, depending on the number of pints he had tanked, either a genius or a fool. He had the kind of conservatism that sprang from having survived two world wars. When he was being really irritating, he would blab the secrets from my confessional to his old mates in the pub.

"That's not the most original of questions," I said.

"But a hard one to answer well," he replied and I heard him scratch his head. I was alone in the middle of a million acres of scrub but I could hear his voice. Your father's voice is one that never leaves you.

"I agree, but I've put some thought into it. I don't see my journeys in the way that other people see them."

"That's obvious," he said. I sensed his impatience. *"So go on, get on with it."* I imagined him taking another sip of his ale.

"The consequences of any action can be good or bad, and it's the future consequences of any of my journeys that make me say they were either satisfactory or not."

"All right, all right. So things are good and bad. You're choosing your words carefully, but you're muddled. It's like sleight of hand..."

"No it isn't. I'm trying to work it out." He was right. I was struggling to make sense of it all. Why don't things show themselves more clearly? Why couldn't I have just written about what was out there, the stuff about who I met, getting laid? Why was I always so edgy, so anxious? I couldn't get through a minute without some bit of introspection, instead of *'how well I cornered round that or this goddamn bend.'* Who cares how I ride my bike? Saying *'I did it because it's there'* doesn't actually answer anything.

"Well go on, have you worked it out yet? Get on with it."

"If you ask me whether I had coffee this morning for breakfast, I can either try and remember whether I did, or I can conduct an experiment, which is what I have done with my journeys. I can make myself believe that I did have coffee and then make myself believe that I didn't. Then I compare the two and decide which is best for me, and that becomes the answer."

If there had been Cuckaburra birds around then they would have cuckaburred. If there had been any saplings of eucalyptus I would have been made nostalgic by their scent.

"What has coffee got to do with around the world biking?" My thoughts were interrupted. He was right. I was talking nonsense. My doubts were echoed by this father voice in my head, the voice of a blond-headed man, hands wiped dry on his knees, a handkerchief by his pint.

"The thing is son that you're at it again, thinking of a complicated answer to a simple question which in your own

words defies simple understanding." He paused. *"Let me put it another way. **What-are-you-on-about?"***

"Simply that I imagined how it might be to bike around the world slowly, and then how it might be to do it fast. When people said that I would see more of the world going slowly than fast, I imagined that if that was true for them then it would be true for me. So I rode around the world slowly, on a slow bike, and then I did it again fast on a fast bike. The first time was on an Enfield with a 500cc single cylinder engine. It broke down every three days, I never went over 55 miles per hour, and it took me seven months to ride 32,000 miles."

"Get to the point."

"Wait, let me finish. It's a long answer, but it might explain things. So I imagined myself doing a world trip on a fast bike, as fast as possible. I thought that I might see less and in the conventional sense of *'seeing'* I really did see less, which could have been bad for me. But then I realised that I had begun to *perceive* more, and that was good for me. When I tried the experiment and actually did the journey, I found it was true. I did understand more, even though because of my tiredness, sleep-deprivation or whatever, I began to see illusions. I saw Corinthian pillars where there were none. I saw honey-kissed rainbow showers that sweetened my skin, when in reality I just got wet. Realness is an illusion anyway, so I was only comparing one illusion with another. Comparing the two, I think it was better that I went fast. I saw more, and even though it was an illusion of my own making, I still saw it. When this ride is over it will become like a dream, and I will have to reconcile all that effort to have a dream about a journey that was an illusion."

"There you go with your pillars....you should have been an architect instead of an adventurer, son."

"Maybe I didn't actually see them, but I got fed up with seeing places as they were. With Calcutta looking like an armpit and smelling like a drain, I just drew another picture of it in my head."

32

It was already past summer in Alaska and into autumn. In a queue of colours the reds and the yellows were waiting for the browns, and they were all on hold for winter. I rode all day along dusty roads that filled my boots with powdered clay. Newly-laid flint flew up beneath the bike, and the tracks made by my tyres were the only sign of my passing. I rode on between scented pines.

The bike sounded sweet, not a beat out of place. The engine purred gently, the sound ricocheting against spindly tree trunks in a valley. The mechanism sounded complete. Every part felt taut. The air whipped around my face. When I looked down, the wind wrapped itself around me differently and the sound changed. I had no thoughts in my head, just the usual images whirling around my burnt-out mind.

"You just want to get laid!"
"No, it isn't like that."

"That's what you all say, you travellers, all wanting to ride along the noble route, head in the clouds, feet not even touching the earthly ground."

I wondered how my alter ego knew me so well. There was a bend, loosely gravelled on the near side. A large black bird flew across in front of me. A car approached. The road straightened. My eyes blinked. I hoped I would keep awake. What was that feeling? It was the longing for something. It was the vagrant in me, the need to wander.

"Describing unfulfilled sexual longing, my dear host, is a neurosis. My dear friend, I give you your ideas. It is me, not you, that tells of the adventure and the wandering. You just think you do. I give you your thoughts. Adventure and wandering are, as Freud said about myth, the distorted wish-dreams of entire peoples."

Where had all this come from? Another bend. The trees parted to show a thin stream that, come the thaw, would turn into a raging river. A car passed. Another bend. Straight again. A road stained with greasy marks. I looked to the road ahead, but my moist eyes blurred the view. Fatigued beyond fatigue, I was going to have to stop.

"What was that? Something to do with Freud?"
"C'mon! Everyone knows about Freud!"
"I only know that his stuff was based on outdated beliefs, derived from a small unrepresentative group of neurotic Austrian women having a collective menopause."
"Oh, very knowledgeable. You know nothing!"

"For an alter ego you're bloody rude."

"So what! Time is warped space and if you tread on a banana skin you'll go head first down a worm hole and that's it - reincarnated in another dimension as a Danish pastry."

What was I doing? This conversation was keeping me awake, but it was also pointless. Had I just created this character to stop myself falling asleep? Frost heaves on the road threw me up and down like a rider in a rodeo show.

"Look, all I know is that we are half-rational animals pretending to be children of the gods, and somewhere along the tightrope between dream-wishes and cataclysm there is a clue about what to do next. Maybe journeying is one way to find out."

"I remember something that happened when I rode round the world a couple of years ago," I started to say. My eyes closed. It seemed a long time before they opened again, and I was still upright. I caught myself beginning to skew across the centre of the road. The rush of adrenalin stoked up my senses and my thoughts kicked back in.

"You told me. You were on a country road in Pennsylvania, two days from New York. A woman followed you. She said that she had to have you. So you parked your bike, got down to your knees, put your head in her lap, then slowly stood upright against her hitched-up shiny pink skirt, pushed her back on to the bonnet of her car, squeezed yourself between her legs and fucked her."

"Well..."

"But that's all right, eh?"

111

"Well, yes, but you're making me blush. Anyway, how do you know that?"

"I know everything about you. You saw her again in Austria, behind the Opera House. I remember you thinking how ugly she was on a second viewing and how could you possibly shag her, but that it was too late to back out...such a decent guy."

"I was out of order. Anyway, how do you know that?"

"I know things about you that you don't know yourself. It's all right, you're human. But don't you see... I am you."

"What kind of an alter ego are you?"

"I'm you. Everyone's got their own and I'm yours. You've let me out of the bag. You've levered open your Pandora's Box, you've asked the questions and now your very own three-headed beastie has come out to haunt you."

A loud shrill sound came from somewhere nearby. It sounded like a railway station intercom echoing around the trees.

"Oh yes, everyone has one. I am the weightlessness of your thoughts and the heaviness of being that you have to carry around. I am your real unrealness. I am you, or at least the you that you didn't know you had. It's a nightmare having one of me in your head. Pass it on, tell your friends, be the life and soul of your party. A legend in your own head-space."

There was something impish in my thoughts. It was true that in the half-light of a late afternoon one summer, years ago, I had sunk to my hilt in an unknown woman against the bonnet of her car. These chaotic thoughts inside my helmet occupied my attention for the next hour and a half. I thought about all the breasts I had ever known. Once in San Francisco I had met a girl whose breasts were so big that if they had been unstrapped in anger they would have registered on a seismograph. *'If yer wanna see my nice big titties boy yer gonna have ta feerk me.'* Oh dear, if I must. So stuck on the memory of nipples wider than the rim of a tea cup, I rode my bike for eighteen hours across America.

It was not restful thinking. It had become uncomfortable. Somewhere between the pornography and the need to come up for air I rode and I rode, straddling the animal between my legs whose cry rose to a roar between gear changes and settled down to a purr on long stretches of highway.

"What is it that you search for when you go so far for so long?"

"Go away."

"No, go on. What is it that you search for when you go so far for so long?"

I switched off. I saw only the road ahead of me. Long straight sections undulating with more frost heaves that buckled the tarmac. Ravens and bald eagles, brown bear and moose. My concentration faded. I began to worry that I would hit a caribou in a herd chasing across my path; that I would startle them from hiding in the dense avenues of pine trees that came down to both sides of the road. The Alaskan wilderness was all around; high mountains with glaciated peaks; rivers of frozen water making new valleys, cut off at the alluvial plains.

I didn't stop between gas stations. The sound of my engine rumbled through my helmet, penetrating my leathers and vibrating through my body just enough to let me know that I was still moving. I saw beauty. I felt tiredness. Hunched over the tank, I breathed quietly and rhythmically to the sound of the machine. My mind was blank. I was at peace. At last I stopped in a layby to sleep for ten minutes.

"Go on then. What is it that you search for when you go so far for so long?"

"No, fuck off. Let me sleep."

"Oh charming. Fuck off yourself."

There was a monster in me that kept me awake and wouldn't go away. As if shouting to the world, I screamed out across the valley:

"The taste of death ahead of me." The words did not echo. They were wrenched from my guts.

*"So you **do** know,"* said a voice in the wind.

33

The road I was on followed the Matanuska River. The Talkeetna Mountains in the north descended from the Alaskan Range to the road and continued as the Chugach Mountains in the south. The Glen Highway wound through dense trees. I saw brief glimpses of the river. It was midsummer in Alaska and the days were warm, though it was freezing cold at night. Past Tolsona Creek I saw a signpost for Glennallen. The few stores I had stopped at for provisions were closed. I was suddenly tired again. It was as if my energy drained like a baby; one moment demanding the attention of the world, the next indifferent to its own existence. But always I had to go on, until fatigue forced me to rest.

I stopped on the outskirts of Glennallen and drove into the car park of the Caribou Hotel. It was midnight in the light of an Alaskan summer, three weeks away from the longest day. I was told that the US-Canadian border had closed early, and I would have to hang around in the cold. This information was incorrect, and I wasted time sleeping when I should have been riding through the night.

"Preserve and reserve; be cool," I told myself. I tried to remain calm about the schedule I had set up.

The hotel at Glennallen was built as a large mountain lodge on the edge of a forest, off the road. I took a small room and slept, dreaming about my make-believe life in which I rode like the wind, ran like the cougar within me across the plains, and flew like the eagle within me across the sky.

Diary: Glennallen, Alaska, to the Alaska Hotel, Dawson Creek, BC
I am another day's ride farther down the Alaskan Highway and I am too out of my mind to write much. I am going to lie in my bed in the Alaskan Hotel and stop thinking. My head

has gone critical, and that's interesting. I am in Dawson Creek in British Columbia, at the Alaska Hotel and Dew Drop Cafe. Charles, my friend from the last time through, has created one of the nicest small hotels in the world. I love it here and don't want to get up tomorrow. It's raining.

I rode north-west to Glennallen, on to Tok, turned south-east on to the Alaskan Highway, then crossed into Canada at Beaver Creek. On to Whitehorse and into the Yukon. I had two hours' sleep in someone's shed at Johnson's Crossing. Through the night to Teslin. On past Trapper Ray's by Laird hot springs, and on through long stretches of roadworks, slipping on the dust and the slime, riding on loose gravel for hours. Every view was draped in a sharp clear wind.

34

Jung made a detailed study of Chinese, Amerindian, Greek, Roman and Indian gods and goddesses, demons and divinities, animisms, totems, ancient symbols and mythological motifs. He found that these primitive mythological images appeared in similar forms in the dreams and the fantasies of civilised modern Europeans, who were not consciously aware of such knowledge and had not acquired it during their lifetime. For many people in India, day-to-day life is inextricably entwined with the notion of destiny, represented by *aide memoires* of figures and statues painted in bright colours. Mythological symbolism may, like inherited innate structures, be archetypes common to all people. The journey, or the quest, is one of them.

In tales of journeys of all kinds, *'once upon a time'* should read *'once beyond time'*, for it is there that the journey really happens. A wild rage pulses in me as a reminder of how easily I could be imprisoned by the sort of life that would force me to smash and bite. Mythology remembers the innocence of the first state: the perfect virtue of the Taoists, Adam in the garden; that a characteristic of men in the Golden Age was always to be migratory.

And what did they see, these travellers along the highways? Apocalypses and earthquakes? Most people co-exist peaceably and accept their lot, but this is not newsworthy. So travellers become gatherers of controversial information. This has always been so. Marco Polo was an emissary for the Kublai Khan. Columbus was for the king of Spain. So strong is the migratory impulse that a mother bird will abandon her fledglings rather than miss the appointment for the long journey south. Kierkegaard said "There is no thought so burdensome that it cannot be walked away from."

35

Last night I felt depressed about the whole project. Sometimes I feel I am alone, and wonder if anyone cares. Why was I trying to break a speed record? Why climb Everest? Why climb it in the winter? Why take the most difficult route? Why climb without oxygen? Why bother?

'There the eye goes not, speech goes not, nor the mind. We know not, we understand not how one would teach it.' In the past I have gone away and come home again, and only my Dad and I have known I've been away. As he, my great oracle, used to say, 'Sit down son and eat yer chips before they get cold, and you can tell yer mother all about it later.' There was never a later.

36

Past drab Whitehorse, pretty Muncho Park, and the summit lake. Somewhere I saw a lake that was covered in iridescent green ice. It was so beautiful but I rode on: it was the only way. Then in front of me a small herd of caribou galloped across the road. The surface was loose gravel and to brake would certainly have brought me crashing to the ground. The animals ran from left to right, and I tweaked my bars fractionally to the left towards the hind legs of the last one, hoping he would not be startled and stop in his tracks. If he did, I would ride into him at eighty miles an hour, unable to stop or slow down. I steered with a touch of my fingertips, and as the herd crossed my path he kept running and I missed him by the width of his shanks.

So close. I must sleep. I'm dead tired. Yet I mustn't. Hour after hour I continued to ride, stopping only for fuel every three hours or so. To sit down for a coffee would finish the day. At least the breeze was cool and kept my drowsiness under control. But at last I could ride no more. I parked in a truckstop at Nanton on the Canadian border and made my way to a table.

I was awakened by a gentle waitress at about four-thirty am. She was like a nurse. It was a Saturday morning and the sun had not yet risen. So tenderly did she wake me from my slumber, and so gentle was her fragrance that she seemed like a fairy dancing in the moonlight.

"It's time to get up, you said you were going around the world," she said. I opened my eyes very slowly, and when I saw her leaning over me I would have walked across hot coals just to rest my face in her bosom for a pillow.

"I want to stay here forever," I said.

"You can't. I've made you coffee. You have to get to the end of where you're going."

"I don't know where that is any more." I looked out of the window. It was still dark outside. "Do you know how far it is to Texas?" She shook her head. "Did you believe me when I said I was biking around the world?"

"I believe what folks tell me, and that's the sum of it."

"What if it isn't true?"

"Makes no odds to me 'cos I won't know. Do you want your coffee or not?"

"Thanks," I said. She poured a coffee and pushed the sugar bowl a little closer. "Have you seen New York?" I asked her.

"All I know is that you can't see it from here. Fact is, you can't see nothing from here because there's nothing to see." She smiled and walked away.

The early morning sun bled the sky of acid blue. Above me, anchored to the air, was harboured a fleet of clouds the colour of slate. Riding the bike is the only constant in my head now, and it's as if nothing else exists. I am riding past the grain silos of the farming cooperatives of Milk River and after that across the Canadian-US border. Soon I am on Interstate 15 to Great Falls, where I take Highway 87 and somehow end up at Billings.

Diary: *Somewhere in Wyoming*
My back tyre is wearing badly. The people at Anchorage only had soft compound tyres in stock, and I am not sure if it will last all the way to Texas. At the airport I thumb through the Yellow Pages and try unsuccessfully to find a Triumph dealer. The other agents are closed. Tomorrow is a Sunday, so I have no choice but to carry on and hope that the tyre won't wear too thin.

I find Interstate 90 and ride on to Ranchester and Sheriden before turning off to a motel in a little village called Midway, 30 miles or so north of Casper. A storm has risen in the Rockies. It has been growing all afternoon. In the late evening it brings great flashes of lightning and rain. I have to lean hard into the wind. It gets worse - or more magnificent. Crashes of thunder and electricity spike the black sky all around me. I feel as if I am in the epicentre of a cloudquake.

In a lightning flash I caught sight of a little animal like a porcupine running towards my front wheel. I was leaning hard into the wind and the rain and I couldn't move off line in time to avoid him. I felt my front wheel hit his little skull and I was so sorry for him as he died. I called it a day and took an exit to Midway, thirty-three miles before Casper, Wyoming.

The woman at the motel told me that she reckoned further south the weather would be impossible for bikers, so perhaps stopping here was a wise decision. I've been riding since four-thirty this morning, eighteen hours. Another 700 miles through two torrential storms, and winds that I thought would lift the bike off the ground. And through major road construction. I can't go any faster and I can't do any more.

37

There is an Eastern tale that tells of a rich magician who had a great many sheep. But at the same time, this magician was very mean. He did not want to hire shepherds, nor did he want to erect a fence around the pasture where the sheep were grazing. The sheep consequently wandered into the forest, fell into ravines and so on, and above all, they ran away; for they knew that the magician wanted their flesh and their skins, and this they did not like.

At last the magician found a remedy. He hypnotized his sheep and suggested to them, first of all, that they were immortal and that no harm was being done to them when they were skinned; that on the contrary, it would be very good for them and even pleasant; secondly he suggested that the magician was a good master who loved his flock so much that he was ready to do anything in the world for them; and thirdly, he suggested that if anything at all was going to happen to them, it was not going to happen just then, at any rate not that day, and therefore they did not need to think about it.

Further, the magician suggested to his sheep that they were not sheep at all. To some of them he suggested that they were lions, to some that they were eagles, to some that they were men, to others that they were magicians.

After this all his cares and worries about the sheep came to an end. They never ran away again, but quietly awaited the day when the magician would want their flesh and skins.

38

It was sunny in Casper and the Chamber of Commerce Tourist Centre was open. I asked a nice lady if I could send my e-mail and stories from here via the Casper gateway. Pert and dark-haired, this lady was so milky, so creamily nice. I asked her how she could be so nice all the time.

"Well thank you kindly sir," she replied, nicely processed by the Industry of Niceness. "That's so nice of you to say so." Her niceness made me want to outrage her, and I wanted to tell her what I thought about her cute little titties. I'm sure she would have smiled and said, "Well sir, my little titties are kind of cute. I'm sure pleased that you noticed them sitting prettily under my cashmere sweater."

"May I use this phone here?" I said instead, pointing across her desk.

"You most certainly can," she said, and brushed against me close enough for me to catch her scent.

"I've seen a lot of oil wells around here," I said, trying to think of some way to keep her attention while she stood real close.

"Yes sir," and she smiled again. "Casper is just a little old ink-spot on the world and that is a fact, but home is home I guess."

Someone came in, a tourist, so I logged on to the Internet. Publishing the story like this allows for only one draft when operating at this speed. What comes into my head as it happens gets written up and published. I was only hanging around to be alone with Miss Inkspot again. I e-mailed my story and then packed up and was ready to go. With one last glance at the contents of the cashmere sweater I jumped on the bike, u-turned to a garage, refuelled and set off south.

Back on the road, a guy in a car in front of me got pulled over by the Wyoming cops. It could have been me. I was doing 75 and he was doing more. The patrol car u-turned, drove across the central reservation, and threw on its lights and siren as if apprehending a serial killer. Oh dear. Time for a coffee and a sticky bun. More cakey food. The diet of the fat people.

Continuing south towards Denver I passed Chevrolets and Mustangs, and watched them struggling with their own cumbersomeness. The fat, puff-cheeked drivers looked as if they were sitting on sofas in their living rooms. No-one leaves more squalor in his wake than a passing millionaire. The ancient Egyptians, with their concept of an afterlife journey through the Field of Reeds, projected on to the next world the journeys they failed to make in this one. Here, they have it all now.

I rode on and on, hour after hour, getting drunk on the distance. Riding out of Cheyenne on I-25 and crossing the I-80, I began to suffer from the heat. Early man was originally a wanderer in the scorching and barren wildernesses of this world and now so was I.

Once, on the edge of the Mohave Desert and descending across the salt flats, I was poised at the lowest point of a landscape that fried in the hot air. For most of us, blank horizons and a dazzling sky clear the mind of distractions, but for the Aborigine or Tuareg, or native American Indian, deserts and plains are not like that; in such places they must develop their orientation and smell and sift a thousand different signs - the ripple of a dune, the way a tree is bent, tracks of a beetle, when rain might fall.

In south Wyoming, amid the flower smells of a departing summer, this journey taught me how every man might meet again those images he once beheld as a child, in the shimmering dream of his future. Childhood fantasies strive for fulfillment; the images are not lost but come back again in the ripeness of time, even at the expense of possessions, former lives, lovers and eventually sanity.

Diary: *If Only the Banana Were Unknown in My Land*

Somewhere near Cheyenne I lay down to sleep on the side of the freeway because I couldn't keep my eyes open any longer. They were closing as I rode. I realise that this story is a simple one about a man who spends his days trying not to do what he wants to do. I had covered so little distance - 250 miles up to that point. Even after half a good night's sleep I was still tired; deep down I was probably exhausted. I slept in the grass in the sun, only to be woken by rain falling on me. It sounds idyllic - biking free down the highway into the sun, no worries, no bills, no relationship stuff to deal with from day to day. Except that it wasn't like that. I tried to get up off the grass verge, knowing that to crack now would surely lose me the record. All the effort wasted. Sponsors dispirited. Income dissipated. Girlfriend leaves home, father says 'I told you so,' friends leave notes on their doors saying 'Only real adventurers welcome here'. No, like travellers before me, I have to come back to court with treasures and fruits. If only the banana were unknown in my land, I would travel to where it grows and return a rich man.

I woke on the roadside in the middle of a storm and saw another biker ride past. I set off, rode on a little way, and then ahead was the same biker who waved me to stop.

"The law in this state is to have your lights on," he told me. "And those grasses you were in are crawling with rattlesnakes."

He introduced himself as Doctor Gregory Frazier and gave me his card which read 'Professional Motorcycle Adventurer'. He also produced a yellow piece of paper with his career details on it. He had written several motorbike books, including one called *'Motorcycle Sex... or, Freud Would Never Understand The Relationship Between Me And My Motorcycle'.*

Greg offered to put me up for the night, but I could only stay for a few hours. He lived in Denver, which was just down the road, so we continued down the freeway through two storms and into the downtown district. After a few stop lights and a couple of left turns, we slowed into a narrow alley, and went into his house.

I was worried about my rear tyre, a racing tyre made of a soft compound rubber which now had less than 500 miles left before it hit the core, and I asked Greg if he knew where I could get a replacement. All the shops were closed on Sunday, and most were closed on Mondays. He said he would see what he could do, and phoned around. The Triumph dealer in Colorado Springs was out. Clem, his mate, who was the BMW dealer in Denver, lived in the flat below Greg, but he couldn't get me a tyre either. I eventually spoke with Boz, my contact in San Antonio, and we fixed something with the Kawasaki dealer in Amarillo, who would be open tomorrow. I would get there after I'd ridden through the night. There was always the Triumph dealer in Lubbuck, Texas, but that was a bit far. It was going to be tight.

Greg meanwhile had gone to the kitchen to make me a cup of tea. I looked around the room without moving from my seat. It was an extensive library, expensively shelved, containing books on indigenous peoples of America. Greg told me he was from the Crow tribe in Montana. He had jet black hair adorned with feathers, a long groomed pony-tail, strong hands, eyes like blackcurrants and a face that looked as if it could drink all night and wake as fresh as a lemon in the morning.

This man and I were strangers, but I felt at ease enough to sleep for an hour in his house in a reclining chair. When I awoke, there was a meal of lamb chops waiting for me on the table. I ate it and sucked noisily on the bones.

Only after another cup of tea did we start to chat. I was in good spirits and felt revived, partly by the food but mostly by the company. It was an absurdity of this adventure that I was surrounded by people, but was almost always alone. In the desert of my travelling I was starved of human contact.

I mentioned the parable about the sheep and the magician to Greg. Though he lived in Colorado he was from Montana, just down from his ranch near the Black Hills, so he would surely appreciate it.

"Oh yeah," said Greg, "that little nugget. Why hell, that's the guy who talks about some cosmic catastrophe where two pieces were knocked off the earth and became two satellites, or something like that...is that the one?" He paused. "It was something like a moon and a smaller moon, yup, that was the one."

I didn't care what he said, it was just nice to talk and listen. Out of the window the sun was going down behind the mountains and the shadows were lengthening. We were quiet for a moment, then Greg, obviously still thinking about the subject in hand, broke the silence.

"Yeah, I remember reading about this some time ago, some crazy kind of guy from Az-bek-as-tan or some goddamn place, he talked about how the satellites had to be fed by food sent from earth in the form of a cosmic ray manufactured by humans, and that is the reason for the existence of man."

I was pleased that we had made a connection. So I wasn't the only one thinking such things when my head was cooped up in a helmet all day. Clem came into Greg's study. He was the house-sitter who had come to stay and never left. Clem was reedy-looking and gentle. Did we want more coffee?

Around the room were Greg's life trophies - a picture taken with President Carter, his poems, pictures of bikes. I had glanced at a garageful of classic bikes on the way in. A red Indian sat on a stand.

"Maybe you'd read me one of your poems?" I asked.

"Sure as hell will." He thumbed through a volume called *'Biker Poet'* which he pulled off the shelf. "Yup, I reckon you'll like this one." He chuckled to himself, cleared his throat and recited.

"Sometimes I hate my motorcycle helmet,
Especially when it's hot and I am stopped in traffic.
Inside my brain bucket my brain feels
Like eggs frying up to be an omelet
Another time I hate my motorcycle helmet is when I
Sweat
Or when I want a cigarette.
As much as I hate my motorcycle helmet

It becomes very fond to me
When I see a bee
At 70
And on my helmet face shield
It goes SPLAT!
Then I love my protective head hat."

The coffee arrived. "You know, going back to what you said earlier, there were other things I liked about that guy, and I guess it's because I like eccentrics, but what was he called, *Get-it-off* or was it *Gerd-ge-off* or something? Anyways, he reckoned that the only way the human race could be saved was if everyone had a new organ implanted into them whose sole job was to remind people of the inevitability of their own death." He paused. "Now what was it he said? A short line about the principles of limitation. What was that goddam line?" I waited for him to remember. "Oh yeah, that's the one. "There is a definite time, a definite term, for everything. Possibilities for everything exist only for a definite time."

"You know, I'm a bit suspicious of the cleverness of such things," I said to Greg. "I mean, one philosopher says one thing, the other says another."

"That's life, I guess," said Greg.

"Okay, but what if an alien came down to earth and saw a man in armour? You know, a really complicated bit of kit for the time. The alien's going to think he is a robot or some omnipotent being."

"So?" Greg poured me another coffee.

129

"So, to ride around the world on a superbike in a suit of dynamic-looking red leathers and a helmet makes me look like an alien doing some kind of ground exploration of planet Earth, especially in remote parts of India, when in fact it's just me - you know, Nick the ordinary chap, dressed in an extraordinary way."

"So no point speculating about whether something is true, but more about why something is thought to be true in the first place?"

"I reckon," I said sipping my coffee. I was excited at meeting someone who shared my need to play with the words I'd saved up all day. "I really don't want to go," I said. "I feel I've met a kindred spirit and that makes me feel less alone."

Greg smiled. "But the road is the highway of life, my friend and people like you and me have to travel on it. And if you want to make New York via San Antonio in four days you'd better get going."

Diary: Denver, Colorado to San Antonio, Texas
I am racing against the clock. Have phoned home and have just heard that I've slipped to a 33 day schedule and risk losing the record. I have to bring it back to 32 days to be sure of having the Guinness Book of Records accept it.

The last time I biked into Denver I was on my Enfield. I had reached the outskirts of Denver as I pulled off the freeway and I had cruised into a garage to refuel. When I kicked up to go there was no compression. I tried again, but it was no good. The exhaust tappet rod was short, its top end stuffed up the backside of a valve that was obviously incorrectly seated.

"Tom will sort you out," the garage man had said. "He'll get you going, he's a cylinder head specialist, lives round the corner."

The following morning at his place, Tom told me that because I hadn't adjusted the main jet when crossing the Continental Divide at 11,000 feet, the valve seat had been overworked and had overheated and welded to the head.

Tom said to me over a beer that last time, "You know, the way I see it, our greatest disappointments are not for what we have nearly done, but for what we certainly haven't done. If you think that work keeps you going and is good for the soul, remember the Haitian proverb: 'If work is such a good thing, then how come the rich haven't grabbed it all for themselves?'"

Diary: Denver to Lubbuck

I am drifting through my thoughts, comparing now with then. I have just ridden through the night from Denver. What seems like only moments later it's noon on Monday and I'm in Amarillo, Texas. I bypassed the Kawasaki dealer. I still have a thin back tyre. I remind myself to check it out with the Triumph dealer in Lubbuck, 100 miles further south. If they think it's OK, I'll push on for San Antonio where Joe Harrison's mob, looked after by Jim and set up by my mate Glen, will service the bike in an hour.

Lubbuck to San Antonio
I bypass the dealer in Lubbuck, Texas, and take a chance with the back tyre. To replace it here will take an hour and I could miss my service at Joe Harrison's place in San Antonio. I keep going. I am riding like a jockey in the Grand National, skipping about at high speed on this machine. The weather is dry and fine, and even though I've been up all night I feel OK. I nap every hour and it keeps me going. I wonder how healthy several days without sleep will be. Still, when I get home I can collapse. I am under pressure to reach New York by late afternoon on Wednesday. If I do that, then the final European leg of the trip will be easier, because I'll be able to sleep on the plane across the Atlantic.

Sometimes I ride with bare knees and I feel heavy, bloated, pollen-carrying insects explode on impact with my skin, dripping their cargo on my legs. I see only the flat lands of Texas. A garage owner I met in Dalhart said that I reminded him of someone who had cycled through these parts about ten years ago. He said the lad was doing it for the second time and that he was from Liverpool. An interesting coincidence. I suggested that it might have been me.

San Antonio, Texas to Jackson, Tennessee
Down Highway 87 to Big Spring and on to San Angelo, Eden and Highway 83. Met Interstate 10 down to San Antonio, on to the Anderson Loop East and off at Randolph Boulevard, and there the lads were waiting for me. They set to work immediately while I checked my e-mails and sent my

story. Glen was looking after me, but I couldn't stay the night. Sadly I had to leave after we had dined nearby. Still, the weather was dry. I left the Triumph dealership in San Antonio at half-past midnight. It was warm outside. I had snatched thirty minutes of sleep on the floor in one of the offices. I was roused from a very deep sleep and I was shaking as I came back to the world. I had been dreaming. The Corinthians were green and dishevelled, although once clean and wholesome. They had to stay like this until one of their people died or married. "We are from the Corinth," one of them said. I was friendly with two of their women. They were not beauties, but it did not matter. No kissing. I hadn't telephoned my Dad. Someone called Mildred lived in a suitcase. I sat astride a motorised beer keg and then someone passed me going the other way on a Sprite can. I didn't know what to make of it. I rubbed my eyes and pulled on my leathers. I was keen to start. This was the penultimate leg, and the part of the journey where I could ride fast again and make up lost time. Failure at this point would be very difficult to bear.

I pulled off the freeway, Interstate 30 east. Somewhere out of Dallas, near Texarkana, shaded by a tree, I slept on the tank. I woke from a deep sleep and then fell asleep again, without realising it, and dreamed, and then woke up thinking I was actually asleep on the bike while it was moving. I jolted, expecting to hit the ground. I was surprised when I looked around and saw that I was still under a tree.

So far I have been power napping since Denver. No, actually, since before Coutts and across Montana, Colorado, New Mexico and now Texas. I have come all the way from Dawson Creek in British Columbia without proper sleep. Last night I slept for an hour on the ground in a gravelled truck-parking lot. Like an Indian magician sleeping on a bed of nails, without feeling the sharp stones. I have covered 500 miles since midnight. There are another 700 miles to go before the next midnight, and then 500 more before noon on Wednesday.

39

Diary: Jackson, Tennessee to New York. Has the Spirit Been Consulted?

I speak to my spirit, the same one that was spotted by the woman in Australia, and ask him for a wake-up call. I hear the sound of trucks grumbling outside. I open up my laptop and plug in my phone. There are 42 e-mails waiting.

E-mail from Jackie the Travel Planner in England

I reckon you must have been around Nashville at the time (22:00 Tues.) so from 01:00 Monday after leaving San Antonio, you've covered 876 miles in 21 hours. Say only 4 of these hours have been non-driving - you've averaged 51 mph for 17 hours. If you drop the bike at NY, 23:00 Wednesday, with 5 hours non-driving, 1 hour lost - different time zone - you need to average 47 mph over the remaining 19 hours. If you drop the bike at NY 08:00 Thurs. am, 9 hours non-driving time, 1 hour time zone loss - you need to average 41 mph over 32 hours. By my reckoning you slept last on Saturday - so from Sunday morning until Thursday morning you've been driving virtually nonstop, covering a distance of maybe 3400 miles (assuming you did approx. 800 on Sunday) in a total of 96 hours. I believe you had about 2 hours rest Sunday during a 3 hour break in San Antonio (only 1 hr. sleep), Mon. night and I guess the same Tuesday night. If you drop the bike in NY Thurs. am 08:00 it puts you on target for 32 days - 20 hrs; then less the 7 hours I'd miscalculated in Bangkok gives you 32 days, 13 hrs

The road is grey like my face. Every biker can wheel his face into the wind. Before I sleep I ask myself if the spirit has been consulted. Has the front desk been informed of my wake-up call, spirit? Oh dear. Am I going mad?

Another 467 miles to go before I reach New York. It is half past two in the afternoon and I'm just about to leave Tennessee for Virginia. It was a relaxing experience, riding down the tollway towards the Holland Tunnel. There were eight lanes of traffic, but they were all going in the same direction. Over the bridge I saw in the distance a dusty old ship, the New York, moored along the Hudson River, tied to her brownstones and the reflections of a sinking sun. On my right I saw the boats in the river, clinking and shining. I felt happy and fresh, even though I'd gone through six days and nights only sniffing at sleep.

In the early hours of this morning I started to nod off while riding and woke with a jolt. This would usually make me get the bike to the nearest rest area and stop and sleep, leaning forward on the petrol tank. Then I would set off again, growling up the road from fast asleep to fast awake in half a minute. This morning it was different. For the second time, when I fell asleep on the tank in the rest area I dreamed that I was still riding the bike. In my dream I was riding along somewhere in Virginia and starting to fall asleep. Then, in my dream, I woke face down on the red tank. But instead of stretching and preparing to ride, I wondered in my dream how long it would take for me to hit the ground. I was bracing for the fall. It was a dream within a dream.

I was in Nasik on the Bombay road to Nagpur. The temperature was nearly 40 degrees centigrade. It had taken a long time to get the bike out of Bombay customs and it was Sunday morning before I got going. There was a long queue of trucks, and about a tenth of the way to Calcutta I put my video camera on the front of the bike to film whatever was happening. It was a nothing sort of day. Then suddenly - and shockingly because it seemed so normal a thing to see after witnessing the aftermath of so many head-on collisions - I saw two people lying on the side of the road, their upper bodies covered by a blanket. They were obviously freshly dead. A policeman stood beside them, guarding them, directing the traffic, being there, waiting for the van, hanging around. He saw my camera and said, "Ahhh... video camera!" I barely heard it as I passed. To him, a video camera was a rarer sight than a couple of traffic fatalities. When I played back the tape later I realised that I had filmed the first time I had ever seen dead people.

Now I was in a cab being driven home from friends in the Soho area of New York. The cabbie was from Peru and we were laughing for some reason.

"I come from yer know, the Incas, and they have not even heard of my race and my history roun' here, yer know?"

"I read somewhere that thirteen percent of Americans didn't know where Canada was."

"Exactly what I say," he went on. "So what do they know about geography? Just nothin'."

"New York is kind of beautiful though. It seems like people don't need to go to the party because the party's already here."

"You're so right man, I mean you can get anythink in this world that you jus'want, I mean jus' anythink, I mean they'd import Machu Picchu if someone would want to buy it, huh?"

We laughed more. I was in great spirits and we exalted the virtues of the city, its central elegance and Times Square exuberance. I spoke about those parts I knew, Spanish Harlem and the Bronx. I had bicycled through them once. I also knew the Upper East Side and Central Park. We spoke of the great changes in his country, and about the Japanese president, and about Quito and the dancing President who jousted with chorus girls, and we laughed again.

"Hell," I said to myself as much to him. "This is great. I'm in a yellow cab in New York, doing what you do in the movies and my journey is nearly over." I started to tell him about the two dead people I had seen in India. I told him about the policeman and how their legs had stuck out from under the blanket, their bloodied socks still covered by their slippers. They had to share an overcoat, and one set of knees was bloodied as well.

"It had just happened," I said, "maybe minutes before I arrived, a head-on collision with a truck." Then suddenly we drove past a man lying on his side in the middle of the street, clutching his stomach. A trickle of blood flowed from him and stained the road all the way to the nearest drain.

"He's dead," I said to the cabbie. "He's been shot, hasn't he?" The cabbie laughed. We were having a great time and he was flattered that I liked New York and that I knew Peru.

"Maybe," he said, and carried on driving.

It was odd that the first time I should talk about my first experience of seeing death I should immediately see it again. I went quiet and didn't say another word. I paid the taxi and made it to the room in my hotel. In my head that night I heard a thousand souls scream.

My sponsors had insisted that I rest properly while the bike was being sorted out by the freighters and I began to understand why. I had become casual about something which had almost become too much. Opening my eyes, I looked out from the 26th floor of a hotel on Times Square, straight on to the lights of the most electric real estate in the world.

I phoned my Dad. He was the only person in the world who made me feel calm. We talked about my dog, my post, whether Henrietta had called, the weather. Most of the time with my Dad on the phone from faraway places was spent listening to him searching for something to write with. I heard it from Kathmandu to Calcutta, from Burundi to Bamako and back, him cursing and shifting the dog from under his feet. "Oh bloody hell. Come on Charlie, shift out of the way. Son," he said, "I've tried to call you back three times but this number isn't any good."

"What did you ring?"

"0121 44..."

"Dad, that's the code for Birmingham, I'm in New York. I've just told you the code three times..."

"Oh, you didn't say that, son." He always said that as well. "Okay, put your phone down."

A while later we chatted and he sounded relieved. He was 83, nearly blind, built like a battleship and drank his home-brew beer until he reached the state of the purple nose. He was the sort of father to whom a son finds it difficult to say how terribly much he loves him. He had a lot to worry about, hoping that his progeny would survive. It was his duty to worry.

I told him that I had only 1440 miles to ride from Lisbon to Calais, and perhaps only 24 riding hours to go. I told him a little about the trip but spared him the details and the blushes. I didn't tell him that I sometimes despaired, wondering how I would get through the long nights without sleep.

Last night I dreamed that I had died, and all my friends were waving to me from a shore. In the distance I saw my father sitting in his chair, rubbing his ankles with his hands. He was smiling at me. "Silly old goat," he was saying in his gentlemanly way. He had a sprig of heather in his hair. One day he had crossed over the long divide, and the only man in my life was gone.

But last night I dreamed that my dead father and I were reunited, walking along this dream shore as we used to walk over the hills in our homeland. We used to ramble across the moors between crags and peat bogs, him a younger man, me just a boy. In the stories he told me, he carried his flask of wine and his pouch of cheese, and there was always a forest harbouring a dark-haired woman who he had to save. We would take the train from the city to the country, leaving mother far behind; just Dad, me and a dog who chased the sheep.

"I'm tired Dad," I would say. "Please carry me on your shoulders." For I would be trailing far behind, with my tongue catching summer flies. And in my dream this was where he'd gone now. Tiptoed across in his stockinged feet. I too sometimes balance on the edge of this long thin divide, tipping back and forth.

The image of my father faded and the wind began to blow, picking up dust and swirling small stones across the road. He was gone. I felt alone and empty, but I was glad that we had talked.

I leave Denver at bedtime and wake again in New Mexico. I lunch in Lubbock, Texas and grab a steak for dinner in San Antonio.

40

I was now only two days away from completing my schedule, but I reached my Triumph pit stop in San Antonio late. It was a fast, effective service that allowed only a snatched thirty minutes sleep on an uncarpeted office floor. I dozed for another ten minutes near Temple on Interstate 35, and hit Dallas at rush hour the next day. The cops here pulled me for riding between the traffic, but they let me off. It took them half an hour to catch me.

I didn't stop on Interstate 30, and after e-mailing more stuff from Hope I made Little Rock by five. I was crossing the Arkansas river when a very fat police officer with wobbling jowls stopped me and said "I nearly gave you a ticket, boy." But he burped instead and told me to queue with the rush-hour traffic like everyone else, before letting me hammer on to get to Memphis by nightfall.

At Jackson on Interstate 40 I was stopped again, but the patrol officer had a sister in England and told me to be careful. Later, I slept for maybe another hour. I bypassed Nashville by breakfast time, and I was stopped again by a detective in an unmarked car. He just loved the bike, and said he had to have a closer look.

My days were now divided up by planned food stops that never actually happened. Dinner time and I was here; supper time and I was a little further on. Perhaps I ate once a day. I think my body had begun to economise on its needs. There is a point when the body is so tired that it begins to break down.

I think it's called 'the death zone'. My focus was well away from my stomach now. Eating had become a distraction.

This morning I read a newspaper story from Covington, Kentucky. A widow on a fixed income was suing a tombstone seller who had repossessed her husband's gravestone when she was unable to make the payments on time. By lunchtime I was in East Tennessee, beyond the Cumberland Plateau and Knoxville. I had coffee in a hotel in Kingsport, a delicate collection of white gable-ended houses with bougainvillea dripping off the porches, and green hills and prettiness all around. I sent more e-mails the nearer I got to New York.

By West Virginia I was riding hard, flashes of speed to catch the setting sun. Or was it rising? Sometimes I didn't know. Coffee and breakfast and dinner and Maryland and Pennsylvania all began to blur into one another and then suddenly, quite unexpectedly, quite absolutely amazingly and so thankfully, I saw in the distance the most recognisable city skyline on the planet. Manhattan was there before me. The collective penis of human architecture, the group phallus of the modern age.

And so, the end of another continental leg of my journey. My projectile, me and not me, everyone else and no-one, of nothing and of all things. Above all else I adored America. I loved the cultural numbness of her people. I had a sense of belonging because for all I didn't know about them, I can say with certainty that they knew nothing about me.

41

I stayed overnight in New York while the bike was being dealt with by customs and crated up at the airport. The bike and I were flown from New York Kennedy Airport to Lisbon in Portugal. One of the conditions imposed by the Guinness Book of Records was that I had to ride across two antipodal points, and the easiest ones for me to reach were Wellington in New Zealand and Madrid in Spain.

I left customs at five in the afternoon and rode across Portugal and then Spain. I reached Madrid surprisingly easily by midnight. I didn't ride into the city centre but circled the peripherique, four miles away, until I reached the exit for Burgos. It was nearly 500 kilometres to San Sebastian, and another journey through the night to St. Jean de Luc. Then I rode 1000 kilometres to Calais via Bordeaux and Paris. In the south of France it was blissfully breakfast time, and the beauty of today was that I didn't have to be home until tea. I rode hard across the plains of central France and motored even harder to Paris.

I rode the final 1527 miles in 23 hours and beat the record for circumnavigating the world by vehicle by nearly a day and a half. This was enough.

Throughout the journey the Triumph had performed with easy excellence. The whole of the bike was certainly greater than the sum of its parts. I had previously known no other bike than my Enfield, which also demonstrated great character in the face of adventure. The Triumph had maintained a simple honesty of function all the way around the world, without a single mechanical fault.

I felt close to the bike, but not in an emotional way. I did not humanise the bike because that would have taken away whatever spirit the steel and spark plugs themselves may have had. Somewhere, pitched within the molecules of metal, there is something that I feel is more than machinery. This is the bond between the bike and me: that this beautiful beast, the red one that kicks ass, shoots dust and dribbles mercilessly between motorists and trees, somehow takes me beyond my dreams to where I come out the other side, and allows me to be original in a world where so much has already been done.

Alexander said in 326 BC: *"This ocean is connected with the Myrcanian Sea for the great Stream of Ocean encircles the earth. Moreover I shall prove to you, my friends, that the Indian and Persian Gulfs and Myracanian seas are all three connected and continuous. Our ships will sail round from the Persian Gulf to Libya as far as the Pillars of Hercules, whence all Libya to the eastwards will soon be ours, and all Asia too, and to this empire there will be no boundaries, but what God himself has made from the whole world."* He invited comments from the officers present and only after a long silence did Coenus, son of Polemocrates, pluck enough courage to speak.

"Sir, if there is one thing above all others a man like you should know, it is when to stop."